DATE DUE

Presidential-Congressional Relations

Presidential-Congressional Relations

Policy and Time Approaches

STEVEN A. SHULL

Ann Arbor

THE UNIVERSITY OF MICHIGAN PRESS

Copyright © by the University of Michigan 1997
All rights reserved
Published in the United States of America by
The University of Michigan Press
Manufactured in the United States of America
♾ Printed on acid-free paper

2000   1999   1998   1997   4   3   2   1

A CIP catalog record for this book is available from the British Library.

Library of Congress Cataloging-in-Publication Data

Shull, Steven A.
    Presidential-congressional relations : policy and time approaches
  / Steven A. Shull.
        p.   cm.
    Includes bibliographical references (p.) and index.
    ISBN 0-472-10832-8 (cloth : acid-free paper)
    1. Presidents—United States.   2. United States. Congress.
    3. Political planning—United States.   I. Title.
    JK585.S55   1997   97-4778
                                                        CIP

Contents

Preface

This book uses political time and policy area approaches to examine contemporary relations between Congress and the president. A primary venue for such relations is roll call voting in Congress, including presidential position taking, controversy and partisanship in voting, and legislative support of presidents' positions. These activities revolve around the adoption of public policy and are incorporated in this volume. In addition, *Presidential-Congressional Relations* examines supposedly independent executive actions (issuing executive orders) as an alternative form of policy adoption by presidents who still must operate within the legislative arena.

Existing measures of presidential-congressional relations have been both praised and damned in the scholarly literature. Some of the criticism surrounds the fact that they are based on roll call votes, where each vote is weighted equally. That and other criticisms are addressed here by the inclusion of a data set of important (major) legislation based upon David Mayhew's widely cited *Divided We Govern* (1992). Because his criteria for inclusion yield so few foreign and defense issues, additional major foreign policy legislation based on Barbara Hinckley's *Less than Meets the Eye* (1994) is also used. This combination of data provides sufficient important legislation to categorize by political time and policy areas.

Three different policy typologies are compared to provide rival explanations of modern presidential-congressional relations. *Presidential-Congressional Relations* incorporates two substantive typologies. First is the two presidencies thesis, first advanced by Aaron Wildavsky. One criticism of the two presidencies notion is that the dichotomy is too crude, thereby ignoring variation that possibly would be evident if more categories were available. Therefore, I also incorporate a policy categorization identified by Gary King and Lyn Ragsdale (1988). Additionally, this book uses a functional classification made famous by Theodore Lowi, initially in 1964 and later amended.

This volume also groups government activities according to political time: by presidential party, by individual president, and by selected year in presidential term of office. All legislation and the subset of important legislation and executive orders are assessed from 1957 to 1994, which allows systematic examination of presidential-congressional activities over 38 years.

Utilizing political time in this volume goes beyond standard treatments of chronology or president as units of analysis and adds a new dimension in understanding presidential-congressional relations.

Presidential-Congressional Relations enhances the theoretical and empirical development of the existing literature in several ways. First, it is important to study which particular policy typology contributes most to understanding presidential-congressional relations. Second, the research also uses combinations of years to assess these interactions. Third, adapting the vote data on position taking and support to major legislation and comparing them to all votes allows better assessment of these activities. The fourth purpose is to more fully understand the nature of vote controversy in presidential-congressional relations. Fifth, this research compares legislative support and executive order issuance across issue areas of public policy. Scholars have not addressed this important executive-legislative linkage. If successful, these endeavors will provide an important data set for use by scholars of presidential-congressional interactions. All in all, a clear need exists for a comparative and rigorous, but also understandable, empirical study of contemporary interactions between the first two branches of our national government.

Acknowledgments

Numerous individuals helped enormously in the production of this volume. I begin by crediting three graduate students, each of whom are coauthors of a chapter in the book. Each took several courses from me and, while I hope they learned something, I learned much from them as well. Brad Gomez and Johnny Goldfinger deserted me for Duke, where they are excelling as doctoral candidates. Tom Shaw remains under my thumb and finds it less easy to escape my incessant demands. These superior students contributed data analysis generally and critiqued an additional chapter as well as coauthoring the chapter that bears their name.

Friends and colleagues at the University of New Orleans and elsewhere contributed suggestions and at least three of them read the entire manuscript: Christine Day, Martha Gibson, and Randall Ripley. I am grateful for their helpful comments and encouragement. Lyn Ragsdale deserves special thanks for providing me with useful data prior to the publication of her invaluable volume of data. I also received six anonymous reviews (from three different publishers), all of which were surprisingly encouraging and supportive of this project. They were the kind of reviews that we all hope for but seldom receive for our efforts. Upon deciding to go with Michigan, I am particularly grateful for encouragement from Director Colin Day and Political Science and Law Editor Chuck Myers.

The University of New Orleans provided several services from which I benefited considerably. A coveted research professorship provided a course reduction and a one semester sabbatical leave—both surefire ways to facilitate my productivity. In addition, secretaries Rose Johnson and Regina Pirolozzi helped get the manuscript in shape. During several semesters I had the benefit of competent graduate research assistants: Rachael Wallace and Bobbie Nettesheim (data collection and computer entry), Zachary Fish (references and lists of tables and figures), and Rosalind Cook (proofreading the copyediting and page proofs).

Last and certainly not least, it is a great benefit to be married to a librarian. My wife, Janice, proofread three chapters and helped with data collection and sources. As we near 31 years of marriage, I dedicate this book to her and to our children, Ted and Amanda, who are children no more.

Figures

Tables

CHAPTER 1

Introduction

This opening chapter has several purposes. First, it reviews the extant literature on presidential-congressional relations, illustrating the changing nature of research on this topic. In general, recent scholarship has moved away from viewing the president as the dominant actor in the relationship toward a perspective that sees more equal power sharing between the institutions. Second, the literature and this project are placed into the broader context of such relations, showing that important activities like agenda setting, committee behavior, and other forms of policy adoption cannot be covered in a single volume. Third, the two main approaches used in studying presidential-congressional relations (policy areas and political time) are introduced. Fourth, the research lays out some very preliminary expectations and then explicates the contributions of this volume toward better understanding of presidential-congressional relations.

Research on Presidential-Congressional Relations

The scholarly literature on presidential-congressional relations has grown considerably during the past generation. Much of the early work was descriptive, discussing institutional roles and responsibilities largely in legalistic and/or constitutional terms. This research thought it was most important to see which branch was initiating legislation or formulating policy. Although theories are still in short supply, we now find much more empirical development in the research on the relations between the first two branches of our national government. The emphasis more recently is on adopting public policy rather than on its formulation, often using indicators of presidents' legislative success or support. Although studies relating most directly to decisions that adopt policies are reviewed in this book, just this aspect of presidential-congressional relations alone is broad ranging.

Early Research

Conflicting interpretations exist about presidential power relations with Congress and the relative discretion that each wields. Alexis de Tocqueville, writing in 1835, saw the president "placed beside the legislature like an inferior and dependent power." Fifty years later, in *Congressional Government,* Woodrow Wilson also viewed Congress as dominant. Yet, later in *Constitutional Government,* Wilson himself, and nearly all twentieth-century writers, saw presidential dominance as desirable for our governmental system. However, the United States seemingly limits the "head of government" more than any other major democracy. Upon investigating presidential-congressional power relationships, one finds that the resources and influence of both presidents and Congress are important.

The post–World War II period obviously saw considerable change in presidential-congressional relations. Although earlier presidents had asserted leadership over Congress, Franklin Roosevelt began a pattern of much greater presidential influence that has persisted to the present time. Among other roles, Clinton Rossiter (1956) saw the president as "chief legislator." Richard Neustadt (1955, 1960) and other writers argued persuasively that the presidential era had arrived and that Congress was ill equipped to exert policy leadership. Yet Neustadt also realized the limitations of presidential influence. He asserted convincingly that the essence of the president's political leadership over Congress is his ability to persuade. "All presidents wish they could make Congress serve them as a rubber-stamp, converting their agendas into prompt enactments, and most presidents will try to bring that miracle about, whenever and as best they can" (Neustadt 1973, 136).

Neustadt was not alone in viewing presidents as the dominant actor in the relationship. Early studies attempted to discern which branch initiated major legislation, although authors disagreed over the relative percentages. Thomas Schwarz and Earl Shaw contended that it was less than 50 percent from 1963 to 1972 (1976, 230), but others saw higher figures. Scholars discussing this growing tendency for policy to originate from the executive include James Robinson (1967) and Samuel Huntington (1961). Of course, who initiates policy may have little importance in determining the shape policies ultimately take. The "president preeminent" model soon saw a host of challengers.

Revisionist writers argued that, despite an increasing reliance on the executive for policy initiation, Congress can still play a major role in the process. A classic early study found that Congress was the dominant partner in twice as many issues from 1880 to 1940, although a trend toward presidential dominance during the latter years was observed in the research (Chamberlain 1946). Two writers followed up on Chamberlain's research for the period 1940 to 1967 and found a continued major role for Congress in policy initiation (Moe and Teel 1970). A similar conclusion for the 1950s and 1960s was drawn by James Sundquist (1968). Another observer stated that the "president is often neither the dominant nor the progressive partner in the shaping of domestic policy" (Orfield 1975, 20).

Few writers would go as far as Hugh Gallagher (1977) in asserting that Congress, not the president, is the dominant leader in legislation. Gallagher highlights areas of congressional leadership in domestic policy, including air and water pollution, strip mining, oil price controls, urban problems such as mass transit and land use, employment, banking and commerce, campaign financing, rights of women and minors, crime, economic controls, and taxation.[1] Other writers found that Congress was particularly assertive beginning in the late 1960s and into the 1970s (Fisher 1972).

Congress has exerted leadership in some social programs that reallocate society's resources from the rich to the poor, such as Medicare and child care. More often than not, however, authors found that policy innovations were usually initiated by the executive. Congress was not as responsive as the president to social rearrangement (Orfield 1975, 262). When innovations by Congress on social policy do occur they are generally when Congress has a liberal (and Democratic) cast, particularly following conservative Republican presidents, who showed little inclination for such programs. Thus, Congress plays a more assertive role when presidents are conservative and/or lack political support (Orfield 1975, 261). If Congress initiates less on controversial issues that tend to reorder costs and benefits, it exercises greater input on policies that simply allocate and/or regulate, especially if they are relatively routine.[2]

Congress is not confined to a passive role in policy initiation (Johannes 1972a). Nor does it merely rubber-stamp executive branch proposals. It often modifies such proposals substantially or even rejects them outright. Many bills are introduced without presidential support and receive substantial consideration before the president even takes positions on them, if at all. Although Congress has acquired a reputation for reacting to presidential initiatives rather than enacting its own, a substantial portion of the criticism is undeserved. Liberal Democratic senators have often prodded reluctant presidents, even those who generally are innovative in policy-making.[3] Many earlier congressional initiatives are later adopted by the executive, but Congress retains a firm hand on many others.[4] Diffuse, decentralized relations among committees, interest groups, and relevant bureaucrats allow considerable congressional discretion.

Early Policy Studies

Much of the early literature offers, consciously or not, a policy-content explanation of differences in presidential-congressional relations. Thus, part of the disagreement about relative influence is attributable to policy area differences, which constrain the behavior of both branches. Most authors view the president as more important in foreign policy and Congress as more influential in domestic policy-making. A respected body of literature adheres to the notion that the president "proposes" and Congress simply—rather automatically—"disposes."[5] If this assertion is true, then the foreign policy role of Congress obviously is very different from its substantial power and discretion in domestic policy-making. Functional policy typologies may also help explain relations between Congress and the president.

Substantive Policy Differences
Numerous reasons have been offered for why presidents appear to dominate foreign policy-making (Shull 1979; Fisher 1972). Congress has constitutional powers, but it operates at a clear disadvantage in foreign policy decision making. Writers argue that its diverse and fragmented character makes Congress ill-suited to initiate most foreign policy, often relegating it to reaction rather than initiation (Hargrove 1974, 155; Destler 1974, 85; Donovan 1970). Thus, Congress can exercise negative sanctions by denying support for the president's proposals, but it cannot force him to accept a formal alternative (Hilsman 1968). This view of presidential dominance provides little opportunity for Congress to initiate foreign policy. Indeed, of the 22 foreign policy measures Robinson studied, Congress initiated only 3 and had an influence greater than the president on only 6 (1967, 65). Thus, the view of writers in the 1960s was that presidents have a relatively free hand in foreign policy compared to domestic policy initiation.

This view was propounded by Aaron Wildavsky in the now classic 1966 essay that formed the "two presidencies" thesis, which is utilized in this book as one policy-content approach to presidential-congressional relations. Researchers after Wildavsky continued to find differences in presidential influence over Congress between domestic and foreign policy but generally not the wide diversity Wildavsky observed (Sperlich 1975; LeLoup and Shull [1979a] 1991). If the president has increased his powers somewhat in domestic policy, he has perhaps lost some of his authority vis-à-vis Congress in the realm of foreign policy. In both policy areas, the power of the president in relation to Congress varies over time and issues.

Because the foreign-domestic distinction may mask differences in relations, despite considerable research utilizing this distinction (in Shull 1991), more specific substantive typologies may be desirable. Some authors (e.g., LeLoup and Shull [1979a] 1991; Manning 1977) feel that budget and/or economic issues blur the two presidencies thesis. Indeed, the U.S. economy increasingly is globalized. Others see greater variation within domestic issue areas (Clausen 1973; Kessel 1974) and within foreign categories (Shull et al. 1985; Hinckley 1994). Accordingly, *Presidential-Congressional Relations* also uses a disaggregation of domestic and foreign issues into seven issue areas identified by Gary King and Lyn Ragsdale (1988). (Their coding scheme and an expansion used here appear in table A.1 in app. A.)

Functional Policy Differences

Although most policy research on presidential-congressional relations has focused on substantive distinctions like domestic versus foreign, other literature argues that functional (or analytical) policy areas also distinguish and constrain their relations. In an extensive book review in 1964, Theodore Lowi argued that the type of policy affects politics (the behavior of actors). He saw distributive policies (i.e., agriculture and public works) as being less controversial because they are determined by bargaining among subgovernments (legislative committees, agencies, interest groups) and allocate benefits broadly. Regulatory policies (like crime and pollution) are more contested and involve Congress more as a whole rather than through subgovernments (Lowi 1970). His final functional area was redistributive, which is the most controversial because it involves taking benefits from one group and giving them to another (e.g., shifting tax money from middle- and upper-classes to provide benefits to the poor).[6] Lowi argues that such policies (such as school desegregation and subsidized housing) usually require impetus from presidents.

Lowi developed a fourth category he called "constituent" in his later work (1972, 300). Like distributive policy, constituent policy is characterized by little coercion. This policy category is typified by such issues as reapportionment and creation of new agencies. Because Lowi focused his early attention on domestic policy, many foreign policy concerns (like treaties and the Department of Defense) find their way into the constituent category. Lowi (1972) and Robert Spitzer (1983) view constituent policies as more frequently partisan and centralized. (See table A.2 in app. A for substantive issues categorized here into these four functional groupings.)

Assessment

Presidential-Congressional Relations asserts that the substantive and/or functional content of the policy under consideration affects actor roles, expectations, and behavior. Distributive policy should be more Congress oriented, partly because of the influence of subgovernments, while redistributive issues are more president oriented. The entire domestic policy arena is probably more conflictual than it once was (Wildavsky [1966] 1991; LeLoup and Shull [1979a] 1991; Shull 1979, chap. 10). Therefore, over time, increasing conflict may occur in each of the policy areas, partly because of more direct involvement by both the president and Congress. These actors share power about equally, and domestic and redistributive legislation are primary battlegrounds.

Both Congress and the president focus on their areas of influence and expertise and seek to define issues accordingly. Presidents seem to prefer policies that have broader impact and in which their influence is greatest (Vogler 1977, 317). Reflecting its own interest, Congress tries to transform redistributive policies (such as the 1965 Elementary and Secondary Education

Act) into distributive ones (Lowi 1972, 306). Even conservative members of Congress clamor for distributive programs. Such "bringing home the bacon" is helpful in reelection, while foreign and redistributive policies are less helpful (Fiorina and Noll 1979, 1098, 1101). Thus, domestic and distributive programs are probably the most likely to be adopted. Both Congresses and presidents recognize that power sharing and accommodation are necessary for policy-making to occur in the modern era.

Context of Presidential-Congressional Relations

The state of the nation and the world, public expectations, and partisan control of government are among the many environmental factors that help define parameters for policy-making and shape presidential-congressional relations. The structure of institutions also is important and results in differing constituencies, electoral calendars, and public perceptions of the proper role of each actor. Structure includes particular conditions within both institutions, such as norms, tenure, and degree of centralization. Literature about who initiates legislation has been examined and, thus, agenda-setting leadership and followership are important subjects of study. Such agenda roles occur at many points in the policy-making process, early on as well as during the final decisions that adopt policy. Contentiousness due to increasingly divided government has exacerbated institutional conflict in recent years.

Structure and Environment

The common starting point for studies of presidential-congressional relations is the separation of powers—the division of executive, legislative, and judicial branches in the Constitution. Yet the phrase *separation of powers* is misleading. The Constitution intermingled powers among three branches of the national government and the states, thereby overlapping responsibility for governing. It is more accurate to think of separation of powers, as Richard Neustadt has characterized it, as "separated institutions sharing powers" (1960, 26).

The Constitution also prescribes the structure of government, which plays an important role in institutional capacity. The Founders' decision to share power through checks and balances would prevent tyranny by blocking the accumulation of power by any one branch. This was accomplished by placing institutions in conflict and competition with each other. James Madison, the principal architect of the Constitution, described it in the *Federalist* No. 51 as a system in which "ambition must be made to counter ambition." As the scope of government expanded and the institutional capacity of both the executive and legislative increased, separation of powers sometimes made governing more difficult.

Pre-Floor Activities

Modern presidential-congressional relations are multifaceted. Two important activities occurring early on in policy-making are agenda setting and committee behavior. Because these activities occur prior to policy adoption they are not subjected to extensive analysis here, yet they can clearly set the stage for the later activities on which this volume focuses. Patterns of policy-making in the post–World War II era depend very much on the nature of presidential and congressional agendas. Even when their agendas coincide, each branch may have opposing partisan and ideological goals. One characteristic that stands out in policy-making is its incremental nature. Research shows great stability in agendas, despite changes in officials and policy preferences in both branches of government.

The conventional wisdom paints the presidents in a predominant role, particularly during their honeymoon year in office (Neustadt 1960; Light 1982; Shull 1983). In the area of foreign policy particularly, Barbara Hinckley (1994) argues that the congressional role in agenda setting has declined from its assertiveness in the 1970s. Ronald Moe and Steven Teel (1970) were among the earliest challengers of a presidential-dominant model of agenda setting. Yet, other views see greater power sharing than Hinckley uncovers. Studies show that while assertive presidents can greatly influence the agenda, Congress also can be an important agenda setter (Baumgartner and Jones 1993; Kingdon 1984; Jones 1994, 164). Presidents who push their agenda preferences likely have greater success (Fett 1994; Covington et al. 1995) Still, agenda setting in the current period of American politics is shared, and neither actor appears to dominate the process (Bond, Fleisher, and Krutz 1996, 120).

Another pre-floor activity after agenda setting occurs in the committee stage in Congress. We know little about presidential influence at this stage as Bond, Fleisher, and Krutz (1996) recognize. Richard Fenno (1973) found a greater presidential role in some committees than in others, so policy areas may account for some of these differences. Glenn and Suzanne Parker surmise that indirect presidential influence occurs in committees but that committee voting differs from floor voting (1985). Richard Hall (1987, 117) argues that committee members apparently do wish to support presidents' agenda preferences, especially during the honeymoon year. Studies show that committee leaders support the president's preferences, if perhaps less so than do elected party leaders (Hayes et al. 1984; Bond and Fleisher 1990; Covington et al. 1995). Policy areas relate to pre-floor activities, where distributive policies are more committee-based and redistributive issues are based more in Congress as a whole (Lowi 1964; Ripley and Franklin 1991). All in all, more research is needed on such important pre-floor interactions between Congress and the president.

Presidential-Congressional Relations focuses on the relationships surrounding policy adoption. (For a fascinating case study of such relations prior to policy adoption, see Light 1992.) Policy adoption encompasses floor-voting decisions by Congress, collected by Congressional Quarterly, Inc. (CQ) and widely used in scholarly literature.[7] Other components of policy adoption, such as legislative liaison, budgeting (see Kettl 1992), and the veto (see Spitzer 1988; Watson 1993) are excluded from this analysis.

Current Themes and Concerns

President Dominant?

Most of the early literature emphasizes presidential dominance of the relationship with Congress, particularly in foreign and redistributive policy. Wildavsky's dramatic finding of significantly more presidential influence in foreign policy led to a rash of studies examining this hypothesis following congressional assertiveness in the 1970s. Lance LeLoup and Steven Shull ([1979a] 1991) updated Wildavsky's research and also sought to delve more into subissues within domestic and foreign policy. Lee Sigelman ([1979] 1991) came to widely different conclusions than Wildavsky but used very different data so scholars questioned whether his measures, also collected by CQ, were tapping the same concepts (Shull and LeLoup [1981] 1991).

Two books written in the early 1980s sought to examine presidential-congressional relations more extensively in the domestic policy realm. Spitzer (1983) utilized the Lowi typology and Shull (1983) compared Lowi's with a substantive typology of domestic issue areas to study actor interactions. Both studies found policy typologies enhancing understanding of actor behavior. They observed presidents as more influential in redistributive policies and Congress as more influential in distributive policies. These authors also utilized the CQ boxscore measure of the success of *president's requests* rather than his positions on *legislative votes*. Authors subsequently have relied on variations of these CQ measures.

George Edwards (1980) wrote an important book attempting to explain presidential influence on legislative voting through several features, including presidential election margins and popularity. Like the studies in the late 1970s, he found less presidential influence, even in foreign policy, than Wildavsky observed. Still, Edwards and others saw opportunities for presidents to have considerable influence. Such influence was found by others to exist more in agenda setting and policy formulation (e.g., Light 1982; Shull 1983) than later in the policy-making process.

Congress Submissive?

Literature at the turn of the 1990s argued for diminished presidential influence over Congress, a condition wherein Congress clearly was not submissive, even in foreign policy (Ripley and Lindsay 1993; Peterson 1994). Edwards moved away from his 1980 book on the opportunities for influence toward presidential constraint in his 1989 volume, *At the Margins*. He finds that presidents are not dominant but "are more facilitators than dictators." For Edwards, presidential leadership exists only at the margins, but he believes that margins can be vital for ultimate success with Congress.

Jon Bond and Richard Fleisher (1990) perform more sophisticated multivariate analysis than Edwards's bivariate analysis. Both sets of authors use legislative support for presidents' vote positions as the dependent variable. They use similar variations of support, such as nonunanimous and important votes. Bond and Fleisher find even less presidential influence than did Edwards. They see Congress-centered variables (e.g., legislator ideology) as more important than president-centered variables (e.g., presidential popularity) in explaining legislative support of presidents.

Writing in the same year as Bond and Fleisher, Mark Peterson (1990) develops the most elegant model yet of presidential-congressional relations. Like the others, he finds limited presidential influence and incorporates a "tandem institutions perspective" based on the need for cooperation. Rather than using the CQ support score, Peterson incorporates a modified and expanded version of the CQ boxscore measure (see chap. 6). He then develops an extensive legislative history of the 299 presidential initiatives, offering richer case detail than previously available. Peterson argues that presidents can overcome many barriers to congressional support "by the ways they choose, formulate, and present their policy proposals" (1990, 222).

Divided Government
Another body of literature in the 1990s focuses on the post–World War II phenomenon of divided government, a situation wherein the executive branch is controlled by one party and at least one chamber of Congress by the other party. Although several authors (Cutler 1988; Thurber 1991; Cox and Kernell 1991; Sundquist 1992) have written about the dangers of this situation, David Mayhew (1992) was among the first to challenge the presumption that divided government leads to gridlock in policy-making. He found that both the occurrence of legislative oversight hearings and the passage of major legislation were no different under divided than unified government. Other scholars have found greater effects of divided government (e.g., Cox and McCubbins 1991; McCubbins 1991; Edwards, Barrett, and Peake 1997; Fiorina 1996). These and other authors argue that divided government does encourage greater conflict over legislation, such as increases in the use of the veto (Cox and Kernell 1991).

Mayhew's analysis has been subjected to criticism (Kelly 1993; Goldfinger and Shull 1995) that finds flaws with the methodology he employed. In addition, Mayhew barely discusses a role for presidents. The incidence of major legislation may have nothing to do with conditions facing presidents, such as whether or not they are popular. Charles Jones (1994, 1995) agrees that the president has a limited role in lawmaking. He reminds us in both his recent books that ours is a separated rather than a presidential system of government. Thus, we should expect and not be surprised to find roughly equal power sharing. For Jones, divided government could be more important for direct interactions between Congress and the president than for indirect relations.[8]

Still, the presidential role in adopting policy should not be discounted. Martha Gibson (1995) has embarked on an interesting line of research that examines the effects of divided government on presidents' legislative support using King and Ragsdale's typology. Gibson finds that influence is very much a function of which issue area is of concern. She concludes that divided government seems to have greater influence on broader "cross-cutting" issues of social welfare, government, and resources (also defense to a degree) than on "sector-specific" issue areas of trade, foreign aid, and agriculture. King and Ragsdale also divide executive orders by these policy areas, and this activity by presidents may relate to their legislative relations.

Assessment

The early literature suggested that presidents tend to dominate policy-making, particularly the initiation of legislation. Post–World War II presidents were observed to have considerable resources at their disposal. At the same time, the increasingly decentralized and diffused nature of Congress was felt to limit its policy-making role. But the late 1960s and 1970s particularly saw a less submissive Congress with presidential influence perhaps existing only "at the margins." Some have persisted in the view that presidents are more powerful than Congress in the relationship (Mezey 1989; Spitzer 1993), but others see a more equal (or tandem) basis for presidential-congressional relations (Peterson 1990; LeLoup and Shull 1993). An interesting example of dramatic agenda shift occurred with the election of the 104th Congress in 1994. The major presidential issue of health care had been fought at the pre-floor level during that year, while during 1995 the congressional agenda in the Republican "Contract with America" was fought largely on the floor, where much of it also died.

The Research Problem

Presidential-Congressional Relations uses differences in policy areas and across political time to assess contemporary relations between Congress and the president. Considerable scholarly literature argues that policy determines politics, so aggregating the data by issue area may help explain these actors' behavior. An important venue for such relations is roll call voting in Congress, including presidential position taking and legislative support of presidents' vote positions. These activities are collected by CQ. In addition, this book examines the controversy of such votes (the extent to which they are amended, contested, and/or partisan). Finally, executive actions are examined as a function of presidents' relations in the legislative arena.

These four main activities cover much but certainly not all of presidential-congressional relations. Most of the data rely heavily on legislative voting, which, admittedly, has some limitations (see chap. 3). Nevertheless, these and related notions should help us better understand actor behavior. Such relations probably differ considerably according to how activities are classified, and three policy typologies and political time groupings are compared to provide rival explanations of behavior. None of these conditions for the four activities have been compared or developed adequately in the literature.

Aggregation versus Disaggregation

Presidential-Congressional Relations utilizes both analytical devices of aggregation and disaggregation. Typically, scholars think of case analysis as the least aggregated, while analyzing all data together is the most aggregate form of analysis. Although incorporating aggregation here as a baseline for comparison, most of the data are analyzed somewhere between these two extremes, including grouping data by presidential party, by individual presidents, and by selected years in their terms of office. The utilization of groupings of political time and policy typologies helps explain the rationale for and the advantages of aggregation and disaggregation.

Advantages of Aggregation
One form of aggregation is policy typologies, which provide advantages for both decision makers and scholars. For the former, typologies help to simplify the many and complex decisions they must face on a regular basis. As scholars have shown (see Kessel 1974; Clausen 1973), policy makers, perhaps subconsciously, use policy categories as guides for placing specific issues into an overall ideological framework. Such short cuts allow them to make rapid judgments about their general disposition toward issues. In using typologies thusly, decision makers are thereby using "limited comparisons" rather than making completely "rational" decisions, which would require the impossible task of fully analyzing each issue anew (Lindblom 1959).

Aggregation also has utility for scholars. Like decision makers, political scientists wish to generalize from specific decisions, although the motivations of these two groups are quite different. Scholars seek generalization to obtain a parsimonious theory rather than a quick or consistent decision. They seek to observe patterns of behavior that examining individual cases rarely allows.

Thus, they categorize cases that seem similar in contrast to other categories of cases sharing different characteristics. The grouping into political time and policy areas facilitates generalization.

Using Political Time
In a democracy like the United States, policy-making occurs within a complex internal and external environment. At certain junctures, the political environment is conducive to change, such as the periods following the election of Presidents Roosevelt, Johnson, and Reagan. Some scholars have attempted to discern broader patterns in public expectations for leadership. Arthur Schlesinger Jr. (1986), James David Barber (1980), and James Sundquist (1981) all suggest that American history unfolds in cycles. Schlesinger and Barber argue that public expectations shift from demands for dramatic departures from the past to a period of consolidation to a period of reaction and retrenchment. Sundquist emphasizes the existence of particular cycles in presidential-congressional relations. The greater the public desire for consolidation, the greater will be the influence of Congress and the more constraints the president will encounter.

It would be easy to assert that the eighteenth and nineteenth centuries are characterized by congressional dominance and the twentieth by presidential dominance. Indeed, that is what Sundquist (1981, 21–36) largely does, but he calls the early period of American history (1789–1860) the era of competition, 1861–1900 the period of congressional ascendancy, and the years since 1901 the presidential-dominance era. Charles Jones has a very different view, admitting that the presidency dominated policy-making in the early portion of the present century, but seeing very little presidential dominance since (1995, 11). Indeed, except for brief periods early in the Johnson and Reagan administrations, Jones believes the post–World War II era is quite balanced, sometimes cooperative, but at other times adversarial.

This review suggests that no simple pattern describes presidential-congressional relations. LeLoup and Shull (1993) examine four patterns that characterize presidential-congressional interactions, including presidential dominance, congressional dominance, cooperation/consensus, and deadlock/extraordinary resolution. When studying four policy areas over a considerable period of time, they find instances of each of the four patterns occurring in each of the policy areas. Following this argument, presidential-congressional relations are very much a function of the policy area being considered and the period in time one is studying. Both aspects are approaches used to study actor relations in this volume.

Although some authors refer to long eras in institutional competition, this book explores short-range cycles of such relations. The products of policy-making (e.g., laws, executive decisions) frequently are measured according to a two-year Congress or a four-or-more-year presidency. However, scholars have observed other cycles of government activities, frequently related to the particular year in the presidential term of office (Neustadt 1960; Light 1982; Shull 1983; Nathan 1983; Kessel 1984; Shull and Gleiber 1995). Hence, important short-term cycles may be explained by groupings of such years in political time.

Contribution to Theoretical Development

The theoretical and empirical development of the existing literature will be enhanced in several ways. First, it is important to study which particular policy typology best helps us understand presidential-congressional relations. If the votes can be categorized reliably and if differences within and across these policy areas are observed, then they represent valid typologies of policy content. If so, then policy content may indeed help explain the politics and, perhaps, even the process of policy-making (as envisioned by Ranney 1968; Lowi 1964). This book will then also be able to observe whether substantive or functional typologies are most useful.

Second, different groupings of years have been shown by scholars to have theoretical and empirical utility. In this study, political time provides valuable controls on the data beyond standard examinations. Obviously, dividing these data by presidential party should reveal major differences in assertiveness, preferences, and congressional reactions to them (Kessel 1984; Shull 1983). Individual presidents also have been shown to vary in their legislative relations (Beck 1982; Shull and Gleiber 1995) over time. Finally, the selected years in presidential terms, while sometimes containing few cases, may be important to behavior. Probably honeymoon years are quite different from other years (Light 1982; Kessel 1984; Shull 1983). All three year groupings can be compared to all years together as a baseline.

Third, the research introduces a new data set, consisting of roll call votes on major legislation, developed from Mayhew (1992) and Hinckley (1994). The Mayhew/Hinckley data are provocative, but passage of major legislation identifies little role for presidents. By adapting the CQ vote data to major legislation and comparing it to all votes, we can more fully assess presidential-congressional relations. Adding the Hinckley data increases the number of foreign and defense votes available for empirical testing beyond Mayhew, thereby ensuring sufficient cases for each of the three policy typologies and increasing the reliability of results.

The fourth purpose is to better understand the nature of vote controversy in presidential-congressional relations. The roll call data for important and all legislation provide many different forms of vote conflict and/or partisanship. Such controversy should relate both to presidential position taking and subsequent legislative support and, of course, should vary by political time, by issue area within and between policy typologies, and by whether all or only important legislation is analyzed.

Fifth, presidents have executive options in policy-making, and such decisions may depend on the legislative environment they face. Presumably, presidents who are highly supported in Congress have less need to issue executive orders. Yet, this "administrative" device may be related to legislative conditions. On the other hand, such actions may depend little upon the legislative environment. This research allows a direct examination of executive order issuance within the legislative arena across political time and issue areas of public policy. Scholars have not addressed this important executive-legislative linkage sufficiently.

Finally, *Presidential-Congressional Relations,* if successful in these endeavors, will provide an important data set for use by scholars of presidential-congressional relations. At present, research relies on CQ, Mayhew, or Hinckley measures separately, or variations thereof, all of which suffer from limitations. Indeed, dissatisfaction with current measures has led to manipulations of them as well as to the utilization of CQ's key votes measure (see chap. 6). None are satisfactory by themselves but, by combining and comparing several of them, potential explanatory power and subsequent research on presidential-congressional relations are enhanced.

Summary and Conclusion

The roles and influence of Congress and the president differ considerably depending upon political time and the type of policy under consideration. Differences across political time and by policy areas should have discriminating value for examining the presidents' activities and for determining the extent to which Congress supports these actions (position taking and support). In addition, policy and time approaches should distinguish differences in the controversy of votes in Congress and whether presidents issue executive orders, perhaps to obtain policy adoption independent of Congress. Only legislative support among the four government activities has received much scholarly attention.

Presidents and Congress have differing interests, perceptions, and powers in each policy area. In general, the president should be more foreign and redistributive policy oriented, while Congress should emphasize domestic and distributive policy as the more important object of its activity. This is because each reflects the area of its greatest influence and expertise. Clearly, Congress today is playing a much greater role overseeing executive foreign policy-making than previously. Presumably, it has a greater agenda-setting role, even in foreign policy, than before (Ripley and Lindsay 1993; Peterson 1994; but see Hinckley 1994). It now more frequently defeats presidential initiatives, but presumably rarely initiates, let alone innovates, in foreign or redistributive policy. *Presidential-Congressional Relations* should facilitate an improved understanding of such assumptions.

The final argument of this chapter is that determining who initiates policy is not as important as the recognition that both actors play a role. Roles should vary by political time and policy areas, however, and the content of policy discussed in chapter 2 using typologies may help us understand these interactions. Studying presidential-congressional interactions is crucial to understanding that policy-making function. Both institutions are expected to have influence that varies with the particular activities under consideration, according to the issue area of public policy, and across the particular groupings of political time. All of these conditions may enhance and constrain the relations among the first two branches of our national government.

Presidential leadership and/or congressional followership clearly provide an inadequate picture of modern presidential-congressional relations; rarely is either dominant or submissive. Increasingly, divided government does make institutional conflict more likely, but policy deadlock is not inevitable. Neither actor completely sets the agenda on its own, and cooperation is nearly always necessary for agenda ideas to be adopted subsequently. Yes, presidents are more influential in agenda setting then they once were, but Congress continues as the dominant actor in adoption. The challenge for presidential-congressional relations in the twenty-first century will be to avoid policy gridlock that threatens democratic governance.

CHAPTER 2

Policy Typologies

with Johnny Goldfinger

Nature of Policy Typologies

The policy typologies approach is based on the theory that policy content "structure[s] the interests involved and help[s] determine the political arenas in which decisions are contested or made" (Spitzer 1983, xiv). As a result, variations in the content of policies under consideration produce variations in the roles and behaviors of actors. Scholars have suggested that differences in policy content can be substantive (Clausen 1973; Kessel 1974; King and Ragsdale 1988) or functional in nature (Lowi 1964; Froman 1968; Salisbury and Heinz 1970; Edelman 1974).

The idea of a policy typologies approach has inspired several different strategies for examining the relationship between the president and Congress in public policy-making. In this chapter, the three different typologies used in the book are reviewed. First, the dichotomous "two presidencies" thesis of Aaron Wildavsky is considered. Then, the seven more specific Gary King and Lyn Ragsdale issue areas of domestic and foreign policy are discussed. Finally, after looking at these two substantive typologies, Theodore Lowi's functional typology is examined. The analysis of each approach summarizes its development, assesses and critiques implications of the relevant studies, and ultimately judges the empirical utility of each typology.

Introducing Substantive Policy Areas

Two Presidencies
Wildavsky ([1966] 1991) used a substantive two-part grouping of policy to establish his two presidencies thesis. He maintained that presidential influence with Congress differs so much in foreign and domestic policy that there are, in effect, two presidencies. During the past thirty years, this thesis has been subject to numerous theoretical and empirical arguments and interpretations. The literature has developed to such an extent that an entire collection of research on the two presidencies has appeared (Shull 1991). Up to this point, much of our

understanding of presidential-congressional relations in the post–World War II era has been guided by cumulative research on the two presidencies.

Wildavsky's classic article argued that examining such policy differences provides important opportunities for comparison, which he felt was lacking in much of the literature on the presidency. His quantitative study (using the CQ boxscore) found that Congress supported the president's foreign policy initiatives 70 percent of the time compared with about 40 percent for domestic policy. Wildavsky noted that while often frustrated in the domestic sphere, determined presidents did not fail on *any* major foreign policy issues. That assertion may have been true at the time, but Congress has at times thwarted all later presidents.[1]

Thirteen years later, Lance LeLoup and Steven Shull ([1979a] 1991) updated Wildavsky's data through 1975 and found that the difference in presidential success had narrowed from 30 percent to 9 percent (55 percent in foreign policy to 46 percent congressional approval of domestic initiatives). They agreed that foreign policy usually overshadows domestic policy, but when LeLoup and Shull looked at issues *within* both domestic and foreign policy, they found considerable variation and also the intrusion of economic issues into both domains, thus blurring the distinction between them.

Jeffrey Cohen ([1982] 1991) found presidents more successful in foreign policy since 1861, implying that the two presidencies phenomenon identified by Wildavsky is not just a post–World War II occurrence. However, the 1970s led to a reappraisal of the desirability of a strong president in foreign policy. Congress undertook numerous initiatives to limit the president. Besides greater constraints, a blending of foreign and domestic policy issues occurred. Donald Peppers ([1975] 1991) was the first to suggest a decline in the domestic-foreign policy distinction, and subsequent research showed presidents receiving less foreign policy support in the 1970s than in the 1950s.

As opposed to the CQ boxscore, Lee Sigelman ([1979] 1991) and Harvey Zeidenstein ([1981] 1991) used CQ's key votes to test the two presidencies thesis. In so doing, both authors found more limited differences than did earlier research. However, because their measure is so different both conceptually and empirically from the original, some have questioned the appropriateness of the substitution (Shull and LeLoup [1981] 1991). Chapter 6 discusses the problems and prospects of the various CQ measures.

Later researchers used CQ's support rather than their success measure (see chap. 6), adding other considerations to the thesis, such as variation by party, member status, chamber, and ideology. Zeidenstein found chamber important, while for George Edwards ([1986] 1991), party rather than chamber or even policy is the explanation for the observed differences. Richard Fleisher and Jon Bond ([1988] 1991) found that the two presidencies distinction depends on party and works for Republican presidents only. Thus, a host of challenges appeared.

Ronald Reagan's tenure with its sometimes divided congressional majorities revived the two presidencies phenomenon, thereby questioning Edwards's ([1986] 1991) assertion that it is time bound to the period before the 1970s. Fleisher and Bond ([1988] 1991) wrote the first of a series of articles at least partially reconfirming the two presidencies thesis. Authors writing in the 1990s using varied data sets also found a continuing two presidencies effect.

Terry Sullivan (1991a) argued that the two presidencies distinction is more about winning than support. His analysis uses a new data set composed of presidential head counts (see chap. 6). These data provide a source of information related to but different from the legislative support data commonly used for testing the two presidencies thesis. Head counts offer a varied and possibly more detailed picture of the political process leading up to what is observed in floor voting. Using these data, Sullivan discovered important domestic-foreign differences very similar to those uncovered by Fleisher and Bond.

However, just as scholars were finding a reemergence of the two presidencies, the originator of the thesis began to question its validity. Writing in *Society* magazine, Duane Oldfield and Wildavsky ([1989] 1991) contended that the president's influence in foreign policy has diminished because of several changes: foreign policy increasingly dominates the president's agenda; it has become more partisan and ideological; and, most importantly, it has become more complex. Despite mixed empirical evidence, the authors assert that the two presidencies effect may no longer exist, if it ever did. They state that foreign policy has become more similar to domestic policy.

Despite recanting by Wildavsky, the two presidencies literature continues unabated. James Lindsay and Wayne Steger (1993), for example, argue that the literature possesses numerous deficiencies and suggest remedies for improvement. In response, Shull (1994) points out that many of the problems that these authors mentioned have previously been addressed in the literature. One of Lindsay and Steger's suggestions is expansion of the dichotomy into issue areas. Scholars, however, are already using that approach. A consideration of some of the efforts in that direction follows.

Multiple Presidencies

Many authors have offered refinements to the two presidencies thesis.[2] The consensus seems to be that the two-part typology of domestic versus foreign is too primitive; rather, a continuum or further categories is desirable. Some authors expressing dissatisfaction with a dichotomy of policy advocate further substantive divisions within both foreign and domestic policy (Sperlich 1975;

Shull 1983, 1991; Shull et al. 1985; Hinckley 1994). In response, King and Ragsdale (1988) offer a more detailed division of issue areas for each domain: foreign aid, trade, and defense within *foreign* policy and government/economic management, social welfare/civil rights, natural resources, and agriculture within *domestic* policy.

In earlier works, Aage Clausen (1973) and John Kessel (1974, 1977) come to remarkably similar conclusions about substantive policy dimensions that they observe empirically. Clausen discovered one foreign and four domestic dimensions in congressional voting: international involvement, agricultural assistance, government management, civil rights and liberties, and social welfare. Kessel found the very same ones (plus an additional domestic dimension of natural resources) through a factor analysis of presidential state of the union addresses.

The thrust of these studies has been to reveal more diverse policy preferences than allowed by the two presidencies dichotomy. LeLoup and Shull ([1979a] 1991) and Anita Pritchard (1983) incorporated the Clausen/Kessel dimensions and found that presidential support from Congress varied considerably among the issue areas that they identified. Clausen and Carl Van Horn (1977) showed that the issue areas remain relatively stable, although they did find increased differentiation of the foreign policy domain into aid and defense. Barbara Sinclair (1981) found the same foreign policy differentiations in her study of U.S. international involvement. Another alternative division of foreign policy (economic, security, and political/ideological) was revealed through the factor analysis of congressional roll call votes by Shull and his colleagues (1985). More generally, Martha Gibson (1995) observed variable effects of divided government using King and Ragsdale's (1988) seven issue areas. All of these studies indicate that policy increasingly is becoming more complicated and that substance is an important consideration when studying the behavior of presidents and Congress.

Introducing Functional Policy Areas

Functional typologies purport to uncover analytical rather than substantive bases for political phenomena. The earlier functional typologies were dichotomies: areal versus segmental (Froman 1968); substantive versus procedural (Anderson 1975); and material versus symbolic, depending upon costs and benefits (Edelman 1974). Emmette Redford (1969) added a third dimension by dividing scope of conflict into three categories (from micro to system to macro) to ascertain the degree that interests are represented.

Lowi (1964) began with a three-part grouping of policy content areas and later (1970, 1972) added a fourth category, which Robert Spitzer (1983) defended. Lowi asserted that "policies determine politics," and the most significant political fact about government is that government coerces. "Different ways of coercing provide a set of parameters, a context, within which politics takes place" (1972, 299). The resulting functional typology yielded four distinctive types of policy: distributive, constituent, regulatory, and redistributive (see fig. 2.1). Spitzer noted that "each policy area incorporates its own characteristic political process, structure, elite, and group relations" (1983, 24). Spitzer also claimed that activities in each of the four policy areas differ sufficiently enough to suggest a four-effects model.

Shull (1983, 4) attempted to explain domestic policy formation using three concepts: process, content, and actors. At each stage of the policy process, there was an examination of the relationship between two types of policy content (functional and substantive) and three environmental conditions (individual presidents, party, and year in office). Policy content was posited as the primary explanatory variable in the analysis. Quite different results were found across the two typologies and, as in other studies, there was great difficulty incorporating empirically Lowi's functional typology.

Several other scholars have expanded upon and adapted the Lowi typology. Randall Ripley and Grace Franklin (1991) developed an elaborate model

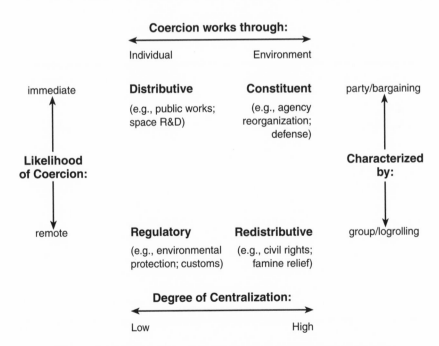

Fig. 2.1. Depiction of Lowi's functional typology. (Adapted from Lowi 1972, 300. For other examples in each issue area, see appendix A, table A.2.)

of congressional-bureaucratic relations in policy-making that they had previously applied to bureaucratic policy implementation (1986). Both their studies use an expanded Lowi scheme, downplaying constituent policy and incorporating the remaining areas in domestic policy but also greatly expanding on foreign policy. They observe three foreign policy dimensions, including structural-distributive, strategic-regulatory, and crisis.

Building Bridges between Substance and Function

At first glance, it would seem that substantive and functional typologies are worlds apart. However, the different typologies can be related as aggregations or disaggregations of each other (see table 2.1). The purpose of this table is not simply to show that some categories can be subsumed within others, but to suggest the existence of common conceptual ground. Table 2.1 summarizes the relations between the various substantive and functional typologies from the extant literature.

Theoretical Structure of Policy Typologies

Substantive Approach to Policy Content

Wildavsky's thesis asserts that "the United States has one president, but it has two presidencies; one presidency is for domestic affairs, and the other is concerned with defense and foreign policy" ([1966] 1991, 11). Furthermore, the president has much greater power over foreign policy as opposed to domestic policy. This dominance exists because "foreign and domestic policy are shaped in distinct policy arenas marked by quite different political configurations" (Oldfield and Wildavsky [1989] 1991, 181).

The derivation of this thesis is based, in part, on post–World War II developments in the public policy environment. "To Wildavsky, the key to presidential power in foreign policy [lies] . . . in changes that had taken place in the world since 1945" (LeLoup and Shull [1979a] 1991, 37). In formulating his two presidencies thesis, Wildavsky ([1966] 1991) identifies four basic conditions that help explain why the president has accumulated vast power in foreign policy: exigencies of the Cold War, speed of modern events, formal/informal powers, and weakness of potential rivals (12–23). From his two presidencies thesis, Wildavsky hypothesizes that the president will be much more successful in foreign policy as opposed to domestic policy. He suggests that greater power and resources in the realm of international affairs will translate into more presidential influence in the nation's foreign policies.

As a test of this hypothesis, Wildavsky examines congressional action on presidential proposals from 1948–64. The data reveal a significantly higher rate of success for presidents in the policy areas of defense and foreign affairs. However, subsequent investigations of the hypothesis have generated mixed results: some researchers are willing to give it partial or qualified support (Fleisher and Bond [1988] 1991; LeLoup and Shull [1979a] 1991; Sullivan 1991a; Zeidenstein [1981] 1991); others strictly limit the applicability of the hypothesis to a particular historical context (Edwards [1986] 1991; Renka and Jones 1991); it has even been rejected (Sigelman [1979] 1991).

Wildavsky subsequently criticized the thesis as being time and culture bound (Oldfield and Wildavsky [1989] 1991, 183). As a result, "things were

TABLE 2.1. Relationships between Substantive and Functional Typologies in the Scholarly Literature

FOREIGN (W)

Foreign and Defense: Structural Distributive; Strategic Regulatory;
   Crises (R & F)
International Involvement (C, K)

Foreign Trade (K & R)
Foreign Aid (K & R)
Defense (K & R)

Foreign Economic (S[1])
Security (S[1])
Political/Ideological (S[1])

DOMESTIC (W)	
Distributive (L, R & F)	Constituent (L)
Price Supports (S)	Government (K & R)
Public Works (S)	Government Management (C, K)
Agriculture (K & R, C, K)	
Regulatory (L, R & F)	Redistributive (L, R & F)
Crime (S)	Civil Rights (S)
Antitrust (S)	+ liberties (C, K)
Resources (K, K & R)	Poverty (S)
	Social Welfare (C, K)

Note:
L   = Lowi's functional policy areas
W   = Wildavsky's two substantive policy areas
S   = Shull's six substantive domestic policy areas
S[1] = Shull et al. three substantive foreign policy areas
C   = Clausen's five substantive policy areas
K   = Kessel's six substantive policy areas
K & R = King and Ragsdale's seven substantive policy areas
R & F = Ripley and Franklin's six Lowi categories

likely different before and after" (Wildavsky 1991, viii). Many of the conditions that were referred to in formulating the two presidencies thesis now are perhaps less influential or nonexistent because the environment in which the president acts has drastically changed (Bond et al. 1991, 197, 199; Peppers [1975] 1991, 27; LeLoup and Shull 1979a; Jones 1995). For example, the Cold War has ended, the president's formal power in foreign affairs has been curtailed, and the number of competitors for control over foreign policy has grown. The two presidencies thesis loses explanatory power as its basic assumptions are undermined by transformations in the conditions and relationships affecting the making of foreign policy.

Functional Approach to Policy Content

Lowi derives a theory based on the idea that government is fundamentally coercive. In his work, he "attempt[s] to identify and derive logically the types of coercion available to governments" (1972, 299). Lowi maintains that policy types can be differentiated by the likelihood of coercion (remote versus immediate) and the applicability of coercion (individual conduct versus environment of conduct). Figure 2.1 presents his ideas schematically.

Spitzer attempts to verify Lowi's theory by deriving and testing hypotheses that model presidential-congressional relations. He states that "the type of policy with which the president deals determines the nature and effects of his political response" (1983, 4). Specifically, Spitzer derives two kinds of hypotheses: one referring to aggregate data and the other to intermediate-level data. His four data hypotheses refer to presidential involvement, presidential influence, the stability of policy types over time, and the number of distributive bills proposed when the president is a candidate for reelection. There are five intermediate-level hypotheses, all of which pertain to congressional roll call voting. These hypotheses posit expectations about the amount of floor activity and partisanship in voting engendered by the policy areas.

To summarize the test results of Spitzer's six hypotheses: one was proved false, one was confirmed, and four yielded ambiguous or inconclusive findings. These results do not provide compelling empirical support for Lowi's theory. However, given that the functional typology appears theoretically sound, the problem may lie in determining the proper classification of policies. Spitzer claims that "policies are categorized according to the wording and interpretation found in the statute itself, not according to the perceptions of the actors involved" (1983, 27). This approach is problematic because a statute in and of itself cannot directly affect an actor's behavior. Actors must first interpret the statute before they respond to it. As such, it is this interpretation that influences their behavior.[3]

Bridging Substance and Function

Shull (1983) attempts to bridge both substantive and functional policy content explanations. Although I found the Lowi functional areas to be quite broad, they provided a useful policy content explanation of domestic policy-making. I identified six differentiated policy areas (agricultural price supports, public works, crime, antitrust, civil rights, and poverty), which can be subsumed within three of the functional arenas. This exercise combined substance and function.

Shull did not list formal hypotheses to be tested but posited numerous expectations across content areas. Many of them are based on Lowi's understanding of the corresponding functional policy type. The six substantive areas considered can also be examined from a functional point of view, with actor roles expected to correspond to those that Lowi asserts for each category. From this perspective, I offered a general hypothesis: "If the typologies are as discriminating as their proponents claim, we should be able to discern differences in each of the policy areas and across time and policy stages" (1983, 26).

Shull then concluded that functional and substantive policy areas help explain the phenomena observed and have both empirical and theoretical utility. I also found that individual presidents, party, and year in office have some influence at different stages of the policy process. Indeed, I considered "policy areas the most important contextual constraint on the policy formation process" (145). Based on this analysis of Lowi's three functional areas, I maintained that they aid in understanding the behavior of actors. Functional areas, for example, were observed to be rather well insulated from the effects of party and selected year. In addition, no distinct patterns appeared in the functional areas across presidents (1983, chap. 6). As for substantive areas, they proved to have "an even greater power to explain the policy process" (155).[4]

Theoretically, the idea of multiple presidencies (whether substantive or functional) makes sense. Differentiating characteristics of particular issue areas may lead to consistent patterns of behavior. Persons take a more active role in the policy-making process when they believe that a particular policy will affect their interests. Various coalitions and interest groups create incentive structures that drive behavior. The assertion that actors distinguish between areas of policy seems to be a reasonable assumption. Therefore, the problem for the researcher is to identify the areas of public policy that best correspond to the perceptions of political actors. The three typologies used here are all based on the theory that policy content has an independent effect on the policy-making process.

Assessing the Use of Policy Areas

Now that the empirical literature using policy typologies has been examined, it is time to decide how useful they are in subsequent analysis. Toward this end, *Presidential-Congressional Relations* takes a more critical look at problems that authors have identified with these typologies. The discussion begins with the substantive typology (the two presidencies), then discusses the functional typology, and concludes with multiple presidencies to build bridges between the typologies. The final section of the chapter advances some preliminary expectations and draws conclusions about their utilization before specific measurement strategies are discussed in chapter 3.

Substantive Typologies

The interpretations to date raise obvious concerns about concepts and measurement and the importance of studying policy content. The two presidencies thesis has endured as an important approach in the study of presidential-congressional relations. Yet, methodological and conceptual problems remain. The general assertion here is that the thesis is more worthy of praise than damnation. But scholars must be more innovative in sorting through the challenges to the two presidencies thesis than they have been so far. Otherwise, it will not endure as a major approach of presidential-congressional relations.

CQ's box score of presidential initiatives to Congress was the database initially used for these first studies. Because CQ stopped collecting these data after 1975, scholars have sought to find different measures to advance research on the two presidencies. Subsequent studies have used *presidential positions on congressional votes* rather than *presidential initiatives,* and so the measures are not directly comparable and often confused (see chap. 6). The emphasis shifted therefore from presidential actions to presidential reactions.

Perhaps researchers have concentrated too much on the congressional venue to study the two presidencies. Oldfield and Wildavsky ([1989] 1991) refer to the need to branch beyond the confines of Congress. The two presidencies could also be associated with elections, where incumbents have greater advantages for manipulating foreign policy than do challengers. Scholars should analyze nonlegislative features (such as executive orders and agreements) and consider subdividing foreign policy into issue areas as with the successful differentiation of domestic issue areas. Both of these strategies are used in this book.

Is the two presidencies thesis still viable? Are there differences between foreign and domestic policy content? The two presidencies thesis has been weakened by the presence of time-bound conditions and the mixed performance of its derived hypotheses (Bond et al. 1991, 192). However, as I stated previously, "although a blending of foreign and domestic policy has taken place, a complete merger will never happen" (Shull 1991, 205). Will any continuing differences between foreign and domestic policy be significant enough to effect the policy process and its outcomes? If the two presidencies thesis is limited by unstable conditions, further division of foreign and domestic policy into issue areas may prove successful. This approach may allow for the use of principles that are better able to model stable environmental determinants.

Functional Policy Areas

Many authors have critiqued and subsequently modified the Lowi typology. Robert Salisbury (1968) argued that Lowi needed a fourth category, which he termed self-regulation. George Greenberg et al. (1977) believe the scheme is important but difficult to test because the basic concepts are not operationalizable. They criticize Lowi for failing to demarcate boundaries. Elinor Ostrom (1980, 198) asserts that the flaws are fatal because the categories are not mutually exclusive. Coding problems were uncovered by both Spitzer and Shull, the latter complaining that issues may change their designations over time (1983, app.).

Other authors complain about the ambiguity of the categories themselves. Faulting Lowi, Marsha Chandler, William Chandler, and David Vogler (1974) argue that typologies, to be useful for further research, must be simple and provide order. In contrast, Peter Steinberger argues that Lowi's typology helps us understand relations between process and content (1980, 185). Douglas Heckathorn and Steven Maser (1990) apply transaction space analysis to the typology, finding that it works better for unidimensional than for multidimensional issues. Virtually all subsequent studies have found the real world more complicated than the typology suggests. Spitzer's (1983) and Shull's (1983) empirical tests of hypotheses derived from the Lowi typology yielded mixed results.[5] Nonetheless, the typology helps provide the basis for theory building and generalization.

Bridging Substance and Function

It should not be surprising that the substantive areas were more successful than the functional ones in my earlier study, which found that classifying policies in the functional typology can be "difficult and frustrating" (Shull 1983, 155). Issues change over time, and the functional categories are not necessarily mutually exclusive. In order to be useful, Lowi's typology requires that actors perceive or expect inherent functional differences in policies. If the researcher is having difficulty determining the function of a policy, then so are the actors. How can behavior be predicted from policy function when the categories are ambiguous?

In contrast, the substantive areas are definitely easier to classify than are functional areas, and they usually offer greater empirical validation. Given that substantive classifications are simpler, there is probably greater consistency between the perceptions of the researcher (the person coding the policy by issue areas) and the political actors (the persons responding to the policy). Consequently, substantive typologies often are better able to group together the policies that have certain inherent similarities that cause actors to behave in a certain way. In the end, "the functional typology [may be] more conceptually elegant but not as operationally useful as the substantive classification" (Shull 1983, 167).

Assessment

Has the blending of foreign and domestic policy eliminated policy distinctions in presidential power? Empirical differences in domestic and foreign policy are still evident, as seen in work by Renka and Jones (1991) and by Sullivan (1991a). So are differences in objectives, organization, personnel, decision making, group support, perceptions, stakes, and ease of implementation. Since such distinctions exist, real differences in the president's impact in the two policy areas are likely to persist. The two presidencies may still be valid, and we are not ready to accept Edwards's conclusion that "there is less to the two presidencies than meets the eye" ([1986] 1991, 115). Some two presidencies research challenges its explanatory power while other studies reveal the emergence of the two presidencies in the 1980s and in the 1990s.

Ultimately, we suspect that a multiple (substantive or functional) presidencies approach has better explanatory power than the two presidencies thesis alone. We make this judgment in part because of limitations observed in the dominant typology explaining presidential-congressional relations. However, it remains to be seen whether the King and Ragsdale or Lowi typologies, or some permutation thereof, offers better explanatory power than does the two presidencies approach. All three policy area groupings are compared in this volume.

Summary and Conclusion

Is Wildavsky, the originator of the two presidencies thesis, correct in recanting it? Has the thesis enhanced our ability to compare presidents and our understanding of presidential-congressional relations? The two presidencies distinction is limited as a theory, but it has and should continue to make a contribution toward our understanding. It shows the utility of a policy approach for studying presidential-congressional relations. Typologies even as simple as the distinction between domestic and foreign policy do encourage such comparison. The two presidencies thesis has endured because it is one of the few attempts in presidential studies to avoid "stylized" facts and examine actual behavior. In addition, it remains an important approach for comparing and understanding, if not yet in fully explaining or predicting, presidential relations with Congress.

The King and Ragsdale typology provides a useful disaggregation to seven issue areas that can be grouped into the two presidencies dichotomy. The categories allow for relatively easy coding (see app. A, table 1). Gibson (1995) suggests conceptual differences among the categories (broad versus narrow effects), lending support to the idea of bridging substance and function within a single typology. Further conceptual and empirical examination of policy areas is needed to better understand presidential-congressional relations.

Spitzer's (1983) analysis of Lowi's functional typology considered floor activity using the number of roll calls for each bill and the number of noncontroversial recorded votes. In testing the effect of policy area on floor activity, a general pattern did emerge, more so with the Senate than the House. Partisan patterns of support were also examined by Spitzer. The test of this hypothesis produced poorer results than the former; he concluded that "partisanship was found to have no particular, consistent relationship to policy types" (147). Similarly, Shull (1983) found some utility in the Lowi typology. It should be noted that no one has tested the typology in presidential-congressional relations using any measure other than CQ's success and support scores.

The chapters that follow compare and contrast the three distinct typologies and their relative influence on government activities over groupings of political time. Ultimately, we expect the multiple presidencies approaches to be more useful for understanding the interactions of Congress and the president. At the same time, all three should have some theoretical and empirical utility. Of course, some of that discriminating value may depend upon breadth of coverage, ranging from the two presidencies to Lowi's four designations to King and Ragsdale's seven issue areas. Chapter 3 operationalizes each of the three policy areas and political time and discusses how they should influence the government activities examined in the study.

CHAPTER 3

Measurement and Using
Important Legislation

Meaning of Presidential-Congressional Relations

This chapter covers the methodology and data (including important legislation) used in *Presidential-Congressional Relations*. It begins by discussing the meaning of this relationship through the public activities of both actors. Private behavior also affects their interactions, but it is difficult to discern and little systematic quantitative evidence exists (Covington 1987). Next, the measurement of the substantive and analytical policy typologies is discussed. Finally, the analysis techniques, using primarily descriptive statistics, are explicated and then the use of political time is examined.

Most of the data incorporated here use some aspect of floor voting in Congress, particularly legislative controversy and support of the president. Presidents' positions on such votes as well as their subsequent nonlegislative actions are also examined. Problems and prospects of roll call analysis are discussed and then adapted to the Mayhew/Hinckley determination of important legislation. Some overall expectations of the research are also introduced. Then, preliminary results of this new data set of roll call votes on the final passage of important legislation are offered. Last, a summary and conclusion serves as a prelude to the data analysis of the four presidential-congressional activities examined in chapters 4 through 7.

Using Roll Call Votes

Much of the existing empirical work on presidential-congressional relations is based upon voting decisions on the floor of Congress. Although a measure of the president's legislative initiatives (the box score collected by Congressional Quarterly [CQ]) was once available, scholars now are largely relegated to examining legislative support or success on votes on which presidents take public positions.[1] Despite the increase in recorded voting in committee decisions, scholars have been unable to identify a clear presidential role until the floor process (see chap. 1). Certainly many bills die before reaching a roll call vote but, at least in recent years, most laws pass with a recorded rather than a voice vote, so a clear public record exists. Of course, a roll call vote need not signify final passage; indeed, it may merely amend legislation. A huge increase in the number of congressional roll call votes beginning in the 1970s offers a rich database for analysis. Most of the increase in roll call votes is due to amendments to legislation, which are often quite controversial (Rohde 1994, 118; Shull and Klemm 1987).

Roll call analysis provides significant benefits but also some problems for the study of presidential-congressional relations. One problem concerns ambiguity in what is being measured. There are differences of opinion about what the indicators drawn from roll call votes mean. Authors allude to differing concepts: "power" (Wildavsky [1966] 1991; Peppers [1975] 1991; Sigelman [1979] 1991); "success" (Bond and Fleisher 1990; Edwards 1985; Hammond and Fraser 1984a; 1984b); "support" (Covington 1987; Edwards 1985; Fleisher and Bond 1983); "influence" (Bond and Fleisher 1980; Edwards 1980; Sigelman [1979] 1991; Mouw and MacKuen 1992; Pritchard 1983; Sullivan 1991b); still others refer generally to presidential relations with Congress (LeLoup and Shull 1979b). Because these concepts continue to remain ambiguous even after scholars have wrestled with them for years, they are discussed more fully in chapter 6.

To better understand the relationship between the president and Congress in the legislative arena, researchers use different groupings of individual roll call votes as either a dependent variable or to create a baseline model. At least ostensibly, concepts like success and support may appear somewhat analogous; however, they should be viewed as fundamentally different (Shull 1983, app.). Some authors use them interchangeably or use success as a dichotomous win/lose measure and use support to refer to individual legislator scores.[2] This section simply introduces each concept and related empirical analyses. Then the advantages of aggregating vote data by political time and policy area are considered.

Although roll call votes contain some pitfalls, they are public, tangible measures of legislative action and appear representative of other behavior (Hammond and Fraser 1984a). Of course, recorded votes are more prevalent in later years than earlier years of the study. One reason is that legislative reforms in the 1970s required recorded votes for most issues, although the number of recorded votes declined somewhat beginning in the 1980s. Second, decision making has been more contentious in Congress, breaking down unanimity that diminishes opportunities for uncontested voice votes (see chap. 5). Scholars disagree over weighting and statistical techniques for analyzing roll call votes (Anderson et al. 1966; MacRae 1970). Even though roll calls are the most visible, they may not necessarily be the most important aspect of legislative behavior. Presidents' legislative liaison and bargaining skills could affect legislative relations, but scholars disagree about how to measure them systematically (Edwards 1989, chaps. 9–10; Bond and Fleisher 1990, chap. 8; Lockerbie and Borrelli 1989; Peterson 1990).

CQ Measures

Beginning in 1945, CQ introduced the box score measure in an effort to tap presidential relations with Congress. Several other indicators were subsequently added (support and key votes), much to the delight of quantitatively minded scholars of presidential-congressional relations. The box score seemingly measures presidential success with Congress. *Success* simply refers to congressional passage of legislation that presidents propose in their public messages. The reasons for success may be serendipitous or otherwise. Contributing to some confusion, CQ subsequently developed yet another measure of success.

In contrast, *support* connotes an alignment with a presidential preference (Pritchard 1986). Success was determined by the proportion of presidential legislative requests identified in their speeches that Congress passes and, more recently, the percentage of presidential vote positions upheld by Congress. On the other hand, support refers to various aggregations of roll call votes by individual legislators. This standard is applied when distinguishing between CQ box scores and support scores (Edwards 1985, 1989; Shull 1983); the former is considered here a measure of success and the latter a measure of support. Distinctions between them and other measures are developed more fully in chapter 6 as is the basis for the decision to utilize support.

Advantages of Political Time

Using political time in this volume goes beyond standard examinations of chronology or presidents as units of analysis. The selected years within presidents' terms of office facilitate the study of patterns and meaning in the relationship between these two institutions both within and across administrations. Four-year presidential terms or two-year congresses exist for a finite length of time, but comparing first, last, and reelection years allows for a more sophisticated and extended discussion. Several studies have analyzed legislative vote data by different groupings of time (Light 1982; Shull 1983). Political time thus adds an important dimension to understanding presidential-congressional relations.

Advantages of Policy Areas

Many studies have analyzed presidential success and support using either cumulative data or using Aaron Wildavsky's ([1966] 1991) domestic and foreign dimensions (LeLoup and Shull [1979a] 1991; Bond and Fleisher 1990; Edwards 1980, 1989). Some scholars have extended this research by using data aggregated into other policy areas or typologies (Pritchard 1986; Shull 1983; Gibson 1995). A policy approach is both valid and valuable. Differentiation by policy areas is nothing new; in the past, they have been constructed on the basis of function (Lowi 1964; Edelman 1974; Froman 1968; Salisbury and Heinz 1970) and substance (Clausen 1973; Kessel 1974; LeLoup and Shull [1979a] 1991). Intuitively, it seems reasonable to assume that presidential support may vary depending on the type policy, which research has verified (Pritchard 1983; Shull 1983).

Given the advantages of the policy approach, Anita Pritchard calls the cumulative data of CQ support scores "a relatively crude measurement of congressional voting decisions" (1986, 481). This book assesses her position that votes should be studied by policy area. It is time to move beyond general measures of support to ones that are more refined, thus allowing scholars to test hypotheses of greater depth and sophistication. A policy approach advances such insight and understanding. Certainly conceptual difficulties and problems with coding exist, but they should not be deterrents. Measurement is improved by advancing rather than ignoring it (Shull 1983, 199). Accordingly, several policy and time groupings are used in this book.

Operationalizing the Policy Typologies

In this second section of the chapter, the specific indicators of the variables included in the analysis are identified. The examination of presidential-congressional relations uses four government activities: presidential position taking, vote controversy, legislative support, and executive order issuance. Because these actions form the basis for the next four chapters on results, their measurement and expectations are presented in each substantive chapter. The operationalizations of the substantive and functional typologies of public policy are discussed here.

The brief one-sentence description of each roll call vote provided by CQ is used to categorize the data into the two substantive and the functional typologies. For a time, CQ differentiated issues into domestic and foreign in the annual editions of their *Almanac* or *Congressional Roll Call* publications. Authors disagree about how particular issues should be classified and also about the more recent decision by CQ to include a separate budget and/or economic category. In any event, categorizing issues into the substantive groupings was rather easy (and into functional categorizations only slightly more difficult) once clear decision rules were established.

Substantive Policy Areas

Because of CQ's changes in categorization over the years, its designation of foreign and domestic is not used. Rather, votes are grouped into the more disaggregated Gary King and Lyn Ragsdale labels and then those seven issue areas are collapsed to differentiate between domestic and foreign (1988, 53). In other words, foreign aid, foreign trade, and defense become the *foreign* category, and government, social welfare, resources, and agriculture become the *domestic* category. The specific issues that are included in each of these two typologies, the broader two presidencies and the narrower King and Ragsdale categorization, appear in the appendix A, table A.1. As shown there, intercoder reliability was well within acceptable levels.

The King and Ragsdale notion that "multiple presidencies" provide better differentiation of relations than does the two presidencies model is evaluated here. However, instances of few cases in certain King and Ragsdale narrower-issue areas occur in some of the years, which can complicate analysis and make results suspect.[3] That is one reason why single years are seldom examined but rather aggregated into the selected year within presidential term or across presidencies and parties to capture more data points. These levels of generality are discussed later in this chapter. Despite limitations, this study further develops King and Ragsdale's categorization, making replication easier for those that follow.

Functional Policy Areas

The data for the functional categories are somewhat more difficult to code. Although Theodore Lowi gives some examples in his various works, he provides "little guidance for determining how a policy is to be classified in any but the simplest cases" (Greenberg et al. 1977, 1534). Not only do some substantive issues fall within more than one category, but issues may also change their designation over time (Wilson 1973, 329; Kessel 1977, 434; Shull 1983; Greenberg et al. 1977; Vogler 1977, 264). The question of issue-area stability threatens the utility of the typology.

Overlap among the substantive issues falling within Lowi's policy types did occur. Several examples illustrate the problems and the gray areas. Health policy can be of at least three different types: distributive if one is referring to subsidies or construction; regulatory if the concern is smoking, pollution, or radiation control; and redistributive when the issue is national health insurance or Medicaid. It could even be classified as constituent if a new agency were created. Welfare policy is normally classified as redistributive, but some instances of each of the other categories were found. A third example is agriculture, where Lowi himself admits considerable overlap across categories (1970, 325). Some agricultural issues, such as the Food for Peace Plan or food stamps, were clearly redistributive and were so labeled.

The present data were classified into the substantive issues that have been identified as fitting Lowi's scheme and expanded upon in table A.2 of appendix A. Analytical characteristics identified by Lowi and others were also used in the coding operation, particularly for those substantive issues not automatically fitting one of the Lowi categories. Other defining features for each policy type, such as the amount of competition, the locus of decision making, the breadth of policy impact, whether benefits are zero sum, and the degree of logrolling were helpful in the classification when the content of the measure alone was an insufficient guide to placement. Despite problems, authors generally agree about the fit of most substantive issues to the functional typology (Ripley and Franklin 1991; Hayes 1978; Lowi 1972; Spitzer 1983; Shull 1983).

All coding by functional area was done by the author, but as a reliability check a graduate student independently coded four randomly selected years. Because the coding was done into discrete categories, not on a continuum, a percentage score is more appropriate than correlation as a measure of intercoder reliability (Gurr 1972, 58). Although there are no particular guidelines for agreement, the 89 percent reported in appendix A is above the commonly used 85 percent agreement level. It should be noted that rather high success in classifying issues may give some credence to these typologies but does not guarantee that they contain underlying theoretical dimensions.

Analysis Techniques and Preliminary Expectations

Statistics Incorporated

Problems of data generation frequently are magnified in their subsequent analysis. Some of the data incorporated here have been analyzed successfully in other contexts. Nevertheless, controlling simultaneously for specific policy areas, political time (such as different administrations), or other narrower concerns greatly diminishes the number of cases available for sophisticated empirical testing. Descriptive statistics are adopted as the most appropriate tools for introducing these preliminary expectations. Thus, means and percentages, such as proportion of position taking by issue area, are most common.

At the same time, simple frequencies are not very useful because differing years exist for many of the aggregations. As an example, just two years are available for the Ford and Clinton presidencies, but eight years exist for Reagan. The number of vote positions taken per year in office is considered, but the primary concern is not position taking overall but relative percentage by policy area. This analysis assesses actor relations only preliminarily using political time and policy typologies, but it does so broadly, and that is an important first step.

Complex analysis, such as predicting activities (position taking, controversy, support, and executive orders) by numerous independent variables, is not offered in this book. That is another book, more along the lines of works seeking to explain a single variable, such as legislative support (see, for example, Edwards 1989; Bond and Fleisher 1990). However, examining four government activities, comparing major and all legislation, and controlling for the content of policy and political time periods provides useful contributions, both theoretically and empirically, for research and greater understanding of presidential-congressional relations.

Using Political Time

The data for this research were collected from a variety of primary and secondary sources for 1957 through 1994. Lyn Ragsdale (1996) generously provided updates on all roll calls and executive orders for her typology prior to publication of her new edition. David Mayhew's data on important legislation are available from 1947 through 1994 in two of his publications (1992, 1995). Mayhew recognizes that the most recent period is not fully compatible with the earlier data.[4] Barbara Hinckley's data begin in 1960, but her coding rules (1994, chap. 2 and her app. A) allow collection of comparable data before and since. Appendix A of this volume also discusses how the May-hew/Hinckley data were adapted. Although year is the unit of analysis, this research is more interested in controlling for the particular units of time discussed next.

Studying political time is important in researching political phenomena. Several scholars refer to a surge and decline in policy making at the presidential midterm, a time when change in congressional seats also occurs (Campbell 1960; Tufte 1978). Hammond and Fraser (1984a) analyze presidential support in Congress by congressional terms rather than by individual years. Such a two-year unit may be the shortest cycle of policy-making. One study of the effects of preferences and resources on activities using two-year Congress as the unit of analysis in civil rights policy-making did not prove superior to analysis using year as the unit (Shull and Gleiber 1995). However, Johnny Goldfinger and Shull (1995) found Congress to be better than year in predicting the incidence of major legislation. Congress as the unit of analysis is an option in future research, but for now year maintains the maximum number of data points.

Grouping years allows for differing levels of generality. These several levels, summarized later in this chapter, range from the most to the least aggregated. The first level looks at each activity across the entire 38-year time period. Such aggregate means allow examining whether general patterns are occurring. For the government activities, overall patterns of position taking, controversy, support, and executive order issuance are provided. Gross differences across policy areas over the entire time period can be observed. Thus, the data are examined overall and then by functional and substantive policy area.

The second aggregation of time encompasses two dichotomies of the data, by party of the president and by periods of divided versus unified government. Comparisons between the two political parties are made to see if the Republican years (1957–60, 1969–76, 1981–92, $n = 24$) differ in emphasis from Democratic administrations (1961–68, 1977–80, 1993–94, $n = $ 14). The divided government years for the 1957–94 period are identical but are kept separate because the executive order data (from 1947) include Truman, who was the only Democratic president to face a divided government until Clinton in 1995. Reagan had modified divided government from 1981–86 when Republicans controlled only the Senate.[5]

Individual administrations are compared to see if the thrust of policy-making has altered over time, both within one administration and across presidential terms. Data for Eisenhower at the beginning and Clinton at the end are limited, but I am able to explore the complete administrations of Kennedy, Johnson, Nixon, Ford, Carter, Reagan, and Bush. Shull and Dennis Gleiber (1995) found that individual presidents have greater effects on government activities in civil rights than do the year-in-term groupings discussed next.

Finally, selected year comparisons are possible. Although fewer data points are available, such an analysis leaves the data in their purest, least aggregated form. Although less amenable to generalization, the comparison of specific policy actions can be observed on a yearly basis. Of particular interest are the first, last, and reelection years within each administration.[6] Such groupings can be reaggregated, thereby capturing more data points. These groupings of political time may be seen in appendix B (codebooks), table B.1.[7]

Expectations

Political time provides an important control for examining actor relations by the content of policy. Overall, the expectation is for greater position taking, controversy, and executive order issuance over time but less legislative support. The extent to which presidents choose to be active in policy-making is a crucial consideration. Also important is whether they desire expansion or contraction of government programs. Either of these preferences implies a change in policy from the status quo. Decision makers seldom offer totally new or innovative ideas; most policy adoption builds heavily from existing programs (Wildavsky 1979, 65). To the extent that policy innovation does mean altering the nation's agenda, however, innovative policies (that is, vigorous actions to expand or contract) frequently occur with partisan or ideological changes in government, or both.

Democrats are consistently the party of domestic policy expansion, while the Republican Party emphasizes contraction or the status quo (Wayne 1978, 19–20; Orfield 1975; McConnell 1976, 44). Certainly this was evident in the Gerald Ford administration. Whether it was due to ideology, Watergate, the growing magnitude of the federal deficit, the uncertain benefits and high costs of the social programs of the 1960s, or growing congressional resurgence, the Ford years generally represented the status quo. For example, Shull (1989) observed that Ford took no vote positions and issued no executive orders on civil rights during two and one half years in office. Ronald Reagan was more active in pushing contractive policies than were his Republican predecessors. Party differences in policy emphasis in Congress and the presidency continue to be important and appear to be increasing (see chap. 5).

A partisan element in the propensity to emphasize particular policies probably exists, and expectations by party have already been suggested. Based upon a wide variety of literature (Orfield 1975; Uslaner and Weber 1975; Fry and Winters 1970; Wayne 1978, 20), a relationship between party control of the presidency and the tendency to emphasize redistributive policies should occur. Specifically, Democratic presidents should emphasize domestic and redistributive/constituent policies (such as civil rights and space programs) to a greater extent than do Republican presidents. Alternatively, Republicans should emphasize foreign (Petrocik 1991) and distributive/regulatory policies (such as agriculture and trade). In an earlier work, Mayhew (1966) sees Democrats as the party of "inclusive" and the Republicans as the party of "exclusive" compromise.

Although parties differentiate among presidents, the individuals themselves are also unique. Indeed, Nathaniel Beck (1982) and Samuel Kernell (1986, 223) believe that policy agendas vary more by administration than by party. We know that Kennedy and Johnson were quite assertive in legislative position taking and Eisenhower and Ford were not. Congress became more contentious during the 1970s, but even greater partisanship and vote splitting has occurred since the 1980s. Legislative support is also highly partisan, with Kennedy, Johnson (and Clinton, for whom limited data are available) faring best, and Ford and Bush faring worst. Finally, executive order issuance is to some degree a recent phenomenon, and its occurrence on a yearly basis should be most frequent for Carter and Reagan. Eisenhower and Ford probably had little inclination to use this device of the "administrative presidency" (see Nathan 1983). Differences across issue areas among the modern presidents should also occur.

Presidents are expected to be more assertive during their first and last years in office and less so during reelection years (Light 1982, 41; Kessel 1975, 9; Shull 1983). Not only are they less assertive during reelection, but they also receive less support from Congress at that time (Wayne 1978, 130). Thus, there should be less congressional acquiescence during presidential reelection years. The reasons for these expectations are simple. Although the first year requires organizing and gaining experience in office, presidents realize they must make their mark early while the honeymoon lasts.[8] Thus, they should be most aggressive then and also when they are lame ducks. During this last year, they have greater freedom of action and presumably wish to leave a historical legacy. Reelection years differ because of their heightened political climate and may give presidents caution (i.e., less assertiveness).

Redistributive/constituent and domestic policies tend to be expansive and to come earlier in presidential terms; the later years of presidents are more frequently characterized by contraction or the status quo (Nathan 1983). Since distributive policies "pass around the pork," it is probably a normal tendency for presidents to initiate them if they are about to leave office or, particularly, if they are seeking reelection. Thus, presidents should emphasize domestic and redistributive policies during their first year and distributive and foreign policies in their last year, especially if they are running for reelection.

Utilizing Important Legislation

Presidential-Congressional Relations contends that important legislation is a valuable subset of all legislation and is worthy of extensive analysis in its own right. It utilizes Mayhew's (1992) operationalization of important legislation, which is combined with an additional subset of important foreign policy legislation compiled by Barbara Hinckley (1994). The roll call vote data collected are comparable to what currently exists for all legislation. This book examines whether important legislation differs from all legislation across policy areas, by political time, and by the presidential-congressional activities used.

Alas, such a comparison is difficult since all legislation contains important legislation and, thus, a whole-part comparison problem exists. Obviously, some of the variance observed in such an analysis of important legislation is shared with all legislation since the respective votes overlap. Accordingly, the only direct comparison of all and important votes is on the first of the four activities: presidential position taking. For the second variable, vote controversy, somewhat differing measures of partisanship are used for important and all roll calls, and voice votes and amendments are included for the former. In examining legislative support, the analysis then switches to all legislation for reasons discussed later. Finally, executive orders, a nonlegislative measure of policy adoption, is incorporated. Next, the prospects and problems of analyzing important legislation are considered.

Advantages of Important Legislation

Roll call votes based on important legislation offer a smaller and thus more manageable data set than votes based on all legislation. Such important legislation votes presumably should eliminate many trivial matters but contain limited numbers, as do key votes (which are discussed in chap. 6). It is also possible to separate out near unanimous votes, amendments, and voice votes as additional measures of controversy on important legislation. The Mayhew/Hinckley data do not tell what happens during the voting process or after legislation passes and offer no role for presidents per se. However, the utilization here of the CQ vote information provides comparable data for important legislation. The important legislation all passed Congress in contrast to CQ's all–roll call votes. Thus, presidents are always supported by Congress when they take a pro position and always opposed when they take a negative position on important legislation. Accordingly, comparing support is more fruitful on all than on important legislation. Nevertheless, roll call votes on final passage of major legislation remain a useful and unique data set.

Disadvantages of Important Legislation

Disadvantages of votes only on important legislation also occur. First, the Mayhew/Hinckley data reveal only major legislation enacted. George Edwards, Andrew Barrett, and Jeffrey Peake (1997) provide a useful analysis of important legislation that did not pass, the denominator that they criticize Mayhew for not providing. They find much greater conflict over important legislation that does not pass than legislation that does during periods of divided government. One could compare these two types of important legislation, but that is not the concern of this chapter. All and important legislation should differ as discussed later.

Several authors challenge Mayhew's designation of major legislation. Mayhew uses two sweeps to identify such laws: sweep one is based on end-of-session wrap-up stories appearing in the *New York Times* and the *Washington Post* as well as journalistic sources. Sweep two draws on long-term perspectives from 41 policy specialists (Mayhew 1992, 37–44). Sean Kelly (1993) and Goldfinger and Shull (1995) are particularly concerned with Mayhew's determinations which are vaguely defined, thereby making replication problematic. As noted earlier, the post-1990 data (consisting only of sweep one) may not be equivalent to that available earlier since no retrospective evaluations are possible.

Assessment/Expectations

One might think that the ideal comparison would be two unique data sets, that is, important versus less important votes. However, such a design is unwise for at least two reasons. First, literally hundreds of roll call votes occur in many years in both chambers of Congress, which would make coding each vote by activity and policy typology onerous. Even more serious, however, is that important and nonimportant votes probably are fundamentally different. It is suspected, for example, that presidents are more likely to take positions on important legislation, which should be more visible than all legislation to the general public.[9]

Even more likely, important legislation may involve greater accommodation on the part of legislators and presidents. Apart from greater presidential position taking, important legislation should be less controversial and less partisan than less important legislation. Although subject to empirical testing, probably too few contested votes would emerge from the nonimportant legislation. It is also important to examine such vote controversy. In short, after some initial comparisons of important and all legislation, both kinds of votes are examined carefully but often separately. Despite limitations on important legislation, a unique new data set is offered (complete with CQ vote information) for scholars to analyze.

Preliminary Results

The next section offers preliminary findings for important legislation, first by the three typologies of public policy and then by the three groupings of political time used in this study. The two tables provide a preview of kinds of analysis used in subsequent chapters but here by examining the number of votes on important legislation rather than the activity variables. These tables divide the roll call data by the two sources of the important legislation used in this research: the Mayhew and Hinckley collections of important legislation.[10] They compare the two data sets giving frequencies of votes according to the political time and policy areas used in this analysis.

Table 3.1 arrays the Mayhew and Hinckley data according to the year groupings. Since differing numbers of years occur in each category, the number of years in each is controlled. Overall, 16.2 roll call votes on important legislation are taken on average each year. Slightly more average votes (2.6 percentage points) appear on important legislation under Democratic than Republican presidents. Table 3.1 also arrays these data by nine contemporary presidents. Here again, year controls are important since only two years exist for Clinton but eight years appear for Reagan. The figures suggest that roll call votes may be reflecting controversy, which is discussed more fully in chapter 5. Table 3.1 shows that the greatest percentage of votes on important legislation occurs under Nixon, Carter, and, particularly, Ford.[11] The fewest votes on important legislation occurred under Eisenhower and Bush, both of whom averaged less than half as many important votes as under Ford. Finally, table 3.1 provides information on roll call votes on important legislation according to year in term. Clearly, the last (lame-duck) year appears to engender a high proportion of important legislation roll calls, but reelection year, which should also be controversial, does not.

Table 3.2 provides frequencies for the number of important roll call votes by policy area, separated according to whether data come from Mayhew or Hinckley. Overall, it is clear that most of the 617 important roll call votes from 1957–94 are based on Mayhew's data, nearly twice as many as for Hinckley. The most dramatic difference by policy area is for domestic and foreign policy. Although there are more domestic than foreign policy votes, as expected, almost all of the domestic votes are from Mayhew while a high percentage (81.8) of the foreign policy votes come from the Hinckley data set.[12] It may also be seen in table 3.2 that while some votes in the King and Ragsdale foreign areas come from Mayhew (particularly trade), the other two areas (foreign aid and defense) are largely from Hinckley. By far, the largest numbers of votes overall occur on defense and social welfare, while the fewest occur in the trade and agriculture issue areas. Finally, table 3.2 reveals the overall frequency of roll calls on important legislation by the Lowi typology.

TABLE 3.1.   Roll Call Votes on Important Legislation (by political time)

Political Time	Mayhew	Hinckley	Total	Number of Years	Number per Year
Overall	405	212	617	38	16.2
By Party					
Republican	242	124	366	24	15.3
Democrat	163	88	251	14	17.9
By President					
Eisenhower	21	27	48	4	12.0
Kennedy	30	12	42	3	14.0
Johnson	69	25	94	5	18.8
Nixon	95	26	121	6	20.2
Ford	34	15	49	2	24.5
Carter	42	41	83	4	20.8
Reagan	65	36	101	8	12.6
Bush	28	20	48	4	12.0
Clinton	21	10	31	2	15.5
By Year in Term[a]					
First	90	51	141	9.1	15.5
Last	57	26	83	3.6	23.1
Reelection	50	19	69	5.8	11.9
Other	208	116	324	23.5	13.8

Source: Compiled from Mayhew 1992, 1995; Hinckley (1994)—latter updated by author; see appendix A.

[a]For important legislation only, selected years can be ascertained more precisely than whole numbers because the actual date exists on which each vote is taken. Note these categorizations by selected year in president's term in the codebooks in appendix B.

TABLE 3.2.　Roll Call Votes on Important Legislation (by policy areas)

Typology	Mayhew	Hinckley	Total
Overall	405	212	617
Two Presidencies			
Foreign	47	211	258
Domestic	358	1	359
King and Ragsdale			
Foreign Trade	24	17	41
Foreign Aid	8	82	90
Defense	15	112	127
Social Welfare	99	1	100
Government	104	—	104
Resources	130	—	130
Agriculture	25	—	25
Lowi			
Distributive	78	—	78
Regulatory	141	9	150
Redistributive	142	86	228
Constituent	44	117	161

Clearly, the greatest number of overall votes occurs in the redistributive area and the lowest proportion (just 11.3 percent) occurs in distributive policy. These frequencies provide useful background for the analysis of important legislation in chapters 4 and 5.

Summary and Conclusion

Considerable debate has arisen over the advantages of various measures of presidential-congressional relations. Certainly there are difficulties with all such indicators, as scholars have documented (Edwards 1980, 50–53; LeLoup and Shull [1979a] 1991, 39; Peppers [1975] 1991; Ripley 1972; 1979, 69; Shull 1979, 1981; Sigelman [1979] 1991; and Wayne 1978, 168–71). No single quantitative measure of presidential-congressional relations is perfect. Qualitative indicators could be just as important, but they are difficult to obtain. The meaning of measures is not always clear; for example, success and support are often confused, as will be seen in chapter 6. Environmental circumstances also intervene, such as the following: Where do the president's and Congress's interests lie? What are their differing expectations? What is the philosophical and/or partisan composition of Congress and the White House? Are the two political branches of government divided or unified by party? At what stage is the president in his term of office? These questions are frequently addressed but seldom resolved in the scholarly literature.

The enormity of the data collection task encourages concentration on a subset of data to analyze whether differences exist in presidential-congressional relations across political time and policy areas. The database consisting of votes on important legislation is small enough to make the data management problem feasible, but there are still sufficient numbers to provide a basis for analysis without trying to categorize every congressional roll call, which from 1976–78 averaged 1,347 votes per year in both chambers combined (*Congress and the Nation* 1981, 7). The analysis also uses votes on all issues, and some comparisons with important votes are possible. Coding of data was difficult but produced results well within accepted limits of intercoder reliability.

This chapter introduced the data on roll call votes on important legislation, comparing the Mayhew and Hinckley sources. Policy typologies, especially the two presidencies, differentiated such votes well. Although about 58 percent of roll call votes on important legislation were in domestic policy, almost all came from the Mayhew data, while the Hinckley source provided most of the foreign policy votes. With respect to the other two typologies, votes appeared more often in resources and redistributive policy and least often in agriculture and distributive policy. Only slightly more votes on important legislation occur when Democrats are presidents, but both the most and least occurred under Republican presidents. Finally, the only political time designation differing substantially from the mean was the last year, where a far higher proportion of important legislation votes occurred than during any other designated year.

Votes will be compared on all and important legislation across political time and policy areas only on position taking. The 617 roll call and 136 voice votes on final passage of important legislation from 1957 to 1994 should allow a direct assessment of controversy by policy area. The many thousands of all votes that occurred in Congress during these years are too cumbersome to permit controversy to be examined in the same way. However, the comparison in chapter 5 of in- versus out-party support for presidents on all votes may also indicate controversy. Finally, legislative support of the president on all votes (chap. 6) and executive order issuance (chap. 7) tap subsequent executive-legislative relations more fully than heretofore.

In sum, *Presidential-Congressional Relations* assesses four government activities and compares a unique data set of votes on important legislation with all roll call votes in the House. The research compares three policy typologies and offers several controls for political time, particularly by political party of the president, by individual presidential administration, and by selected year within presidential term of office. The analysis in the following chapters is not highly sophisticated, but it should tell us whether important legislation, political time, and policy typologies help us to better understand complex relations between Congress and the president.

CHAPTER 4

Presidential Position Taking

Meaning of Presidential Position Taking

Position taking is a discretionary opportunity for presidents to assert leadership in the legislative arena. Presidents cannot introduce legislation in Congress but can express their preferences through this device. Since presidents take positions on a minority of recorded votes, these should be issues of concern to them, where they feel it is necessary to take a stand and when the action could help attain their preferences. Due to the dramatic increase in the number of recorded votes, most significant legislation does come to a roll call vote. Congressional Quarterly, Inc. (CQ) determines whether the president takes positions on a particular vote "by examining statements by the president or his authorized spokesmen" (*CQ Weekly Reports,* January 27, 1996, 239). Position taking and subsequent support thereof are valid and reliable measures for time-series analysis (Bond, Fleisher, and Krutz 1996, 109). Beyond its role in ascertaining presidents' legislative support or success (see chap. 6), presidential position taking itself has not been examined extensively. Position taking on legislation is an important avenue for interaction between Congress and the president.

Presumably, position taking reflects presidential preferences, but such floor vote positions are based on matters regarding Congress's but not necessarily the president's agenda. While such position taking is used to solidify presidents' preferences in the legislative arena, the extent to which Congress actually supports presidential positions reveals Congress's own assertiveness, deference to presidential preferences, and executive-legislative policy congruence. During the legislative process, some of these votes and positions are actually changed as Congress modifies bills from introduction to final floor voting. Although CQ monitors these changes, they are difficult to discern. Accordingly, support (see chap. 6) and related aggregate measures are not perfect indicators of presidents' legislative preferences, perhaps even at the time of the vote. Still, presidents are unlikely to take positive stands on legislation they oppose (Peterson 1990). While many of these roll call votes on which position taking is based deal with executive-initiated measures, they are now in the legislative arena, frequently in revised form. However, such measures seem fairly representative of all roll calls in Congress (Hammond and Fraser 1980, 42).

Measuring Position Taking

Position taking is the number of times CQ records the president as taking a clear public position at some point prior to the vote (*CQ Almanac* 1956, 92). Because it is based on every floor vote on which the president takes a stand, multiple counting may occur on a single piece of legislation. Although some scholars do not like this fact, it is quite possible that the number of roll calls may indicate the importance of the issue (e.g., over a hundred votes on the 1964 Civil Rights Act alone). Numerous votes on a particular piece of legislation may also indicate amendment frequency as an indicator of controversy (see chap. 5). This research examines all of these issues, but the focus in this chapter is on comparing frequency of presidential position taking on roll call votes on important legislation with position taking on all roll call votes. Obviously, since only final passage is used for important legislation votes, multiple vote positions for them are not possible.

However, comparisons can be made on the propensity of presidents to take positions on both important and all legislation as well as by the three typologies of public policy. Comparisons are also made according to political time: presidential party, individual president, and the selected year in presidential term of office. Initially, frequency of position taking per year is presented as well as positions as a percentage of all roll call votes. Subsequently, however, the concern is percentage of positions taken by year and policy aggregations.[1] Obviously, some positions, even on important legislation, are more procedural than content specific, such as Clinton supporting the line-item veto.

Expectations for Position Taking

Presidents take positions frequently on roll call votes in Congress but probably take them most often on votes on important legislation.[2] This finding relates to Gary King and Lyn Ragsdale's argument that presidents do not take positions on trivial issues (1988, 49). Position taking probably has increased over time as presidents increasingly have pursued their policies in the legislative arena. However, position taking as a function of the total number of roll call votes probably has declined. The expectation is that position taking as a percentage of all votes probably increased from Eisenhower through Johnson but then decreased beginning with Nixon as Congress began requiring that most decisions be based on roll call votes. Since the number of roll calls began declining again by the 1980s (Rohde 1994), the proportion of position taking relative to all votes should begin increasing again up through the Clinton administration. The controversial 1995 session produced a record number of roll call votes, with Clinton taking twice as many positions during the second than during the first half of the year (*CQ Weekly Reports,* January 27, 1996, 198). In 1996 he took 59 positions on Senate and 79 positions on House roll call votes.

Position taking may also vary by policy areas, with presidents probably taking positions relatively more often in domestic than in foreign policy because, presumably, more votes occur in the former. Still, position taking probably has increased in foreign policy, but the once greater deference given presidents in the international realm likely has diminished since the congressional reassertion of the 1970s. Within domestic and foreign policy, position taking should also vary by the King and Ragsdale typology. Specifically, presidents should emphasize social welfare and government issues relatively more than foreign aid and agriculture matters. Finally, differences should appear by the Lowi typology, where greater position-taking emphasis may occur on redistributive and constituent than on distributive or regulatory issues. As observed in chapter 2, this expectation is a result of the fact that presidents push the former more because of their perceived greater vulnerability in the latter two areas. Because redistributive and constituent matters probably are more controversial, presidents may feel greater need to assert their preferences by taking positions on such roll call votes.

Position taking probably varies considerably by the political time groupings used in the analysis. Perhaps the most dramatic difference should be by presidential party, where Democrats overall are expected to be much more assertive than Republicans. Obviously, such party differences will also vary by policy area, where Democrats probably emphasize domestic and redistributive policies relatively more, while Republicans emphasize foreign and regulatory policies to a greater extent. Democrats should take positions relatively more frequently on foreign aid, social welfare and resource issues, while Republicans should emphasize defense, government, and agriculture as more worthy of their attention.

Individual presidents probably vary considerably in position taking on legislative votes. From past research, Kennedy and Johnson probably are among our most assertive presidents, and Eisenhower and Ford likely are among the least assertive legislatively (LeLoup and Shull 1993, chap. 3). Also, differences among these presidents should be more pronounced on important than on all legislation. Other presidents likely will be more in the middle on this activity and, of course, emphases will no doubt vary by policy area. Probably Johnson and Ford emphasized domestic position taking while Kennedy and Bush focused on foreign policy.

The final comparison is the year in presidential term of office. Presidents (especially assertive ones) presumably take positions at a much higher level during their first (honeymoon) year than during the last or reelection year. Of course, such position taking by selected year likely also varies by policy areas, where greater attention should be given to foreign and, especially, aid policy during the last and reelection than during the first year. Government and redistributive issues should get more attention during presidents' first years, while regulatory and resource matters may be attended to more during presidents' last years as they prepare to leave office.

Position Taking on Important Legislation

This section of the chapter presents findings of presidential position taking on roll call votes in Congress. The analysis begins with roll call votes on final passage of important legislation identified by Mayhew and Hinckley. These data usually consist of two roll call votes on each measure, one in each chamber of Congress.[3] Position taking is compared across the three typologies and three aggregations of time used in this research. This chapter also directly compares position taking across votes on important legislation and all roll call votes in the House,[4] categorized by the two presidencies and the King and Ragsdale substantive categorizations. For votes on important legislation only, the Lowi typology is also incorporated.

Overall

Table 4.1 provides overall position-taking figures while the subsequent tables group the data by policy areas. In the first column of the table, it is evident that presidents average 10.1 positions on important legislation votes per year in office.[5] Democratic presidents take vote positions nearly twice as frequently on average as do Republican presidents. When looking at the individual presidents, Johnson took an identifiable position an average of 17.4 times per year in office while Reagan did that just 5.1 times per year. These are the two extremes but, not surprisingly given the finding by party just mentioned, no Democrat took fewer mean positions on important legislation votes than any of the Republicans. Finally, from column one of table 4.1, considerable variation occurs in position taking by the selected year in presidential term of office. Presidents average by far the most positions in their last (lame-duck) year as they are about to leave office and average their fewest, by a large margin, during reelection years. Presumably, their reelection effort makes them less attentive to Congress even on important legislation.

The second column of table 4.1 reveals the overall proportion of positions that presidents take as a function of the total number of important votes available. This measure provides a slightly different view of assertiveness in that it controls for the total amount of legislative activity. The first (overall) figure in the second column shows that presidents take positions on 62.2 percent of important roll call votes; here again, Democrats take over 30 percentage points more positions than do Republicans. As mentioned already, the number of roll call votes shot up dramatically during the 1970s before declining again by the early 1980s (Ragsdale 1996). This fact partially accounts for the low percentage of positions under Nixon and Ford but is not the total explanation. Reagan also took positions on a small percentage of important votes even though the relative numbers of roll calls available were fewer than under earlier Republican presidents. Finally, only reelection years reveal a much lower than average percentage of position taking on important legislation votes in both chambers of Congress.

Two Presidencies

The remaining tables reveal presidential position taking on Congress's agenda by policy area. The first column in table 4.2 shows that Republican presidents

TABLE 4.1. **Overall Presidential Position Taking on Important Legislation Votes**

	Overall Frequency X̄ Number per Year	As Percent of Roll Call Votes on Important Legislation
Overall	10.1	62.2
By Party		
Republican	7.6	49.7
Democrat	14.4	80.5
By President		
Eisenhower	5.4	89.6
Kennedy	14.0	100.0
Johnson	17.4	92.6
Nixon	8.2	40.5
Ford	10.0	40.8
Carter	11.8	56.6
Reagan	5.1	40.6
Bush	7.5	62.5
Clinton	12.5	80.6
By Year in Term		
First	9.9	63.8
Last	15.0	65.1
Reelection	5.5	46.4
Other	8.9	64.2

Source: These and all subsequent tables on position taking on votes on important legislation from author's computations based on legislation identified by Mayhew (1992, 1995) and Hinckley (1994), updated by author.

take nearly as many positions overall as do Democratic Presidents; but recall that they also were in office twice as long. Therefore, the purpose of table 4.2 is to show the relative percentages of position taking according to policy area. Overall, 61 percent of the positions are taken in domestic policy compared to 39 percent in foreign policy. As expected, however, Republicans emphasize

TABLE 4.2.   Presidential Position Taking on Important Legislation (by two presidencies)

	Overall (%)	Foreign (%)	Domestic (%)
Overall	100.0	39.3	60.7
	(384)	(151)	(233)
Party			
Republican	100.0	42.9	57.1
	(182)	(78)	(104)
Democrat	100.0	36.1	63.9
	(202)	(73)	(129)
President			
DDE	100.0	67.4	32.6
	(43)	(29)	(14)
JFK	100.0	47.6	52.4
	(42)	(20)	(22)
LBJ	100.0	25.3	74.7
	(87)	(22)	(65)
RMN	100.0	28.6	71.4
	(49)	(14)	(35)
GRF	100.0	55.0	45.0
	(20)	(11)	(9)
JEC	100.0	48.9	51.1
	(47)	(23)	(24)
RWR	100.0	29.3	70.7
	(41)	(12)	(29)
GHWB	100.0	40.0	60.0
	(30)	(12)	(18)
WJC	100.0	32.0	68.0
	(25)	(8)	(17)
Year in Term			
First	100.0	38.9	61.1
	(90)	(35)	(55)
Last	100.0	27.8	72.2
	(54)	(15)	(39)
Reelection	100.0	46.9	53.1
	(32)	(15)	(17)
Other	100.0	41.3	58.7
	(208)	(86)	(122)

Note: Figures in parentheses are base *N*s for the expressed percentages.

the foreign realm to a greater extent than do Democrats, although the party differences are not large.

Table 4.2 shows individual variation among the nine contemporary presidents in position taking in important domestic and foreign policy votes. Obviously, greater variation appears than when just the two parties are examined. Eisenhower's emphasis was overwhelmingly on foreign policy, where 67.4 percent of his positions occurred, compared to Johnson with the lowest percentage, at 25.3 percent. Thus, Johnson devoted three-quarters of his positions to the domestic realm. However, Nixon and Reagan were not far behind him in emphasizing domestic matters. Clinton took positions on numerous important domestic legislation in 1995, including telecommunications, crime, and late-term abortions.

Year-in-presidential-term revealed some surprising differences in presidential position taking on important legislation votes (see table 4.2). Unexpectedly, presidents emphasize foreign policy relatively least during their last year and, therefore, do not appear to seek a foreign policy legacy as they leave office. Alternatively, they push foreign policy legislation much more frequently on average during reelection years. This finding is not so surprising since presidents often find decisiveness in foreign policy helpful during reelection campaigns. An example would be Clinton's support for antiterrorism legislation, which he signed into law on April 24, 1996.

King and Ragsdale Typology

The analysis of position taking on important legislation now shifts to the King and Ragsdale typology, which provides the greatest specificity of the data by policy area. Overall, from the totals row of table 4.3, it is evident that presidents average many more positions on defense and resources matters than they do on trade and, particularly, agriculture issues. Party differences are more striking on the King and Ragsdale groupings than were observable for the two presidencies. For example, within the foreign policy realm, Republicans emphasize defense relatively much more often than do Democrats, but they emphasize trade and aid less often. Within domestic policy, Democratic position taking is greater except on the government/economic management dimension, which was already speculated to be of considerable concern to Republican presidents. Surprisingly, the least partisan difference occurs in social welfare, which accounts for just a .8-percentage-point greater average emphasis by Democrats than by Republicans.

Table 4.3 reveals individual presidential position taking on important legislation votes. Unlike all House votes discussed later in this chapter, disaggregating the data to the King and Ragsdale seven issue areas and also separating the nine contemporary presidents sometimes provides few cell entries. Readers are therefore cautioned against making too many inferences from

TABLE 4.3. Presidential Position Taking on Important Legislation (by King and Ragsdale groupings)[a]

	Overall (%)	TR (%)	AI (%)	DF (%)	SW (%)	GO (%)	RE (%)	AG (%)
Overall	100.0	8.3	11.2	19.8	17.4	16.1	21.1	4.9
	(384)	(32)	(43)	(76)	(67)	(62)	(85)	(19)
Party								
Republican	100.0	7.7	4.9	30.2	17.0	17.6	19.2	3.3
	(182)	(14)	(9)	(55)	(31)	(32)	(35)	(6)
Democrat	100.0	8.9	16.8	10.4	17.8	14.9	24.8	6.4
	(202)	(18)	(34)	(21)	(36)	(30)	(50)	(13)
President								
DDE	100.0	7.0	11.6	48.8	11.6	18.6	0	2.3
	(43)	(3)	(5)	(21)	(5)	(8)	(0)	(1)
JFK	100.0	7.1	28.6	11.9	26.2	14.3	7.1	4.8
	(42)	(3)	(12)	(5)	(11)	(6)	(3)	(2)
LBJ	100.0	3.4	10.3	11.5	17.2	12.6	33.3	11.5
	(87)	(3)	(9)	(10)	(15)	(11)	(29)	(10)
RMN	100.0	2.0	4.1	22.4	20.4	12.2	32.7	6.1
	(49)	(1)	(2)	(11)	(10)	(6)	(16)	(3)
GRF	100.0	10.0	0	45.0	10.0	10.0	25.0	0
	(20)	(2)	(0)	(9)	(2)	(2)	(5)	(0)
JEC	100.0	17.0	23.4	8.5	2.1	19.1	27.7	2.1
	(47)	(8)	(11)	(4)	(1)	(9)	(13)	(1)
RWR	100.0	12.2	0	17.1	19.5	26.8	22.0	2.4
	(41)	(5)	(0)	(7)	(8)	(11)	(9)	(1)
GHWB	100.0	10.0	6.7	23.3	20.0	20.0	16.7	3.0
	(30)	(3)	(2)	(7)	(6)	(6)	(5)	(1)
WJC	100.0	16.0	8.0	8.0	32.0	16.0	20.0	0
	(25)	(4)	(2)	(2)	(8)	(4)	(5)	(0)
Year in Term								
First	100.0	7.8	14.4	16.7	21.1	21.1	14.4	4.4
	(90)	(7)	(13)	(15)	(19)	(19)	(13)	(4)
Last	100.0	9.3	5.6	13.0	20.4	9.3	37.0	5.6
	(54)	(5)	(3)	(7)	(11)	(5)	(20)	(3)
Reelection	100.0	3.1	15.6	28.1	15.6	15.6	18.8	3.1
	(32)	(1)	(5)	(9)	(5)	(5)	(6)	(1)
Other	100.0	9.1	10.6	21.6	15.4	15.9	22.1	5.3
	(208)	(19)	(22)	(45)	(32)	(33)	(46)	(11)

Source: All position-taking data by the King and Ragsdale typology are taken from Ragsdale (1996, table 8.6.).

Note: Figures in parentheses are base *N*s for the expressed percentages.

[a]Legend for King and Ragsdale grouping:

TR	= foreign trade
AI	= foreign aid
DF	= defense
SW	= social welfare
GO	= government
RE	= resources
AG	= agriculture

these particular results. Carter and Clinton gave by far the greatest relative attention to *trade* policy. This is not surprising given that both presidents had visible and important treaties during their terms (e.g., Panama Canal for Carter and NAFTA for Clinton). Somewhat surprisingly, Nixon, who was greatly interested in foreign policy, devoted the least average attention to trade among contemporary presidents. Foreign *aid* revealed very wide divergence in emphasis: Kennedy and Carter taking relatively the most positions and Ford and Nixon taking positions on no important aid votes at all. *Defense* also reveals great differences by individual presidents. Eisenhower and Ford averaged far more positions than other presidents while Clinton and Carter gave it least attention.

Social welfare did not divide the parties much, but Clinton emphasized it relatively more than other presidents, giving more than three times the attention provided by Ford. Indeed, by July 1996, Clinton had twice vetoed Republican welfare reform proposals he called too restrictive. The broad *government* domain does not seem to vary much among individual presidents, presumably due to obligatory matters requiring their attention. Reagan averaged the most positions, probably due to his efforts to deregulate government. *Resources* policy is emphasized relatively more often than any other issue area by contemporary presidents, particularly beginning with Johnson and Nixon, who gave it a third of their attention. Eisenhower and Kennedy gave resources proportionately little attention. Finally, *agriculture* is not emphasized highly by any president except Johnson. Two subsequent presidents took not a single vote position on agriculture.

The year in term also shows differences in position taking by the King and Ragsdale categorization (see table 4.3). Presidents appear relatively more interested in trade in the last years than in reelection years. Perhaps this reflects trade's controversial nature, an expectation explored in chapter 5. The opposite occurs for foreign aid, which, again inexplicably, is attended to relatively more during reelection than last years. Defense is, of course, emphasized heavily during reelections, averaging more than twice as often as during the last year in office. Social welfare shows no difference during the first and last year but is emphasized proportionately less during reelection years. Positions on government matters occur more frequently during the first than reelection years while the opposite is the case for resource policy. Finally, selected year differences are not large for agriculture, but position taking on average is greatest during the last and least during reelection years.

Lowi Typology

The final grouping of position taking on important legislation is by the Lowi typology. Overall, it may be seen in the totals row of table 4.4 that positions are roughly equally distributed across the four categories, with redistributive positions averaging the most frequent (32.6 percent) and distributive the least frequent (15.4 percent). The biggest party differences are in constituent policy, which readers will recall includes many routine government and, particularly, foreign policy matters. Given Republican presidents' foreign policy emphasis, it is not surprising that they focus on constituent issues on average

TABLE 4.4. Presidential Position Taking on Votes on Important Legislation (by Lowi typology)

	Overall (%)	Distributive (%)	Regulatory (%)	Redistributive (%)	Constituent (%)
Overall	100.0	15.4	25.8	32.6	26.3
	(384)	(59)	(99)	(125)	(101)
Party					
Republican	100.0	12.6	23.1	29.7	34.6
	(182)	(23)	(42)	(54)	(63)
Democrat	100.0	17.8	28.2	35.1	18.8
	(202)	(36)	(57)	(71)	(101)
President					
DDE	100.0	4.7	11.6	23.3	60.0
	(43)	(2)	(5)	(10)	(26)
JFK	100.0	23.8	11.9	45.2	19.0
	(42)	(10)	(5)	(19)	(8)
LBJ	100.0	19.5	25.3	40.2	14.9
	(87)	(17)	(22)	(35)	(13)
RMN	100.0	22.4	24.5	28.6	24.5
	(49)	(11)	(12)	(14)	(12)
GRF	100.0	20.0	15.0	15.0	50.0
	(20)	(4)	(3)	(3)	(10)
JEC	100.0	6.4	34.0	27.7	31.9
	(47)	(3)	(16)	(13)	(15)
RWR	100.0	12.2	34.1	39.0	14.6
	(41)	(5)	(14)	(16)	(6)
GHWB	100.0	3.3	30.0	36.7	30.0
	(30)	(1)	(9)	(11)	(9)
WJC	100.0	24.0	52.0	16.0	8.0
	(25)	(6)	(13)	(4)	(2)
Year in term					
First	100.0	17.8	21.1	40.0	21.1
	(90)	(16)	(19)	(36)	(19)
Last	100.0	5.6	42.6	38.9	13.0
	(54)	(3)	(23)	(21)	(7)
Reelection	100.0	6.3	21.9	37.5	34.4
	(32)	(2)	(7)	(12)	(11)
Other	100.0	18.3	24.0	26.9	30.8
	(208)	(38)	(50)	(56)	(64)

Note: Figures in parentheses are base *N*s for the expressed percentages.

nearly twice as frequently as Democratic presidents. The party differences in the other three functional policy areas average only about five percentage points. Although the margin is not large, Democrats do emphasize redistributive policy relatively more (5.4 percentage points) than do Republican presidents, as expected.

Not surprisingly, differences among the individual presidents in position taking are considerable across the Lowi typology, but as with the King and Ragsdale grouping earlier, looking at nine contemporary presidents reduces some of the cell entries considerably. The *distributive* area was emphasized relatively much more by Clinton, Kennedy, and Johnson than by Eisenhower and, especially, Bush (see table 4.4). Clinton also took a far higher proportion of *regulatory* positions than any other president, beating out Carter as the next highest by eighteen percentage points. Kennedy took positions on a higher percentage of *redistributive* policies than any president, suggesting that those who have accused him of caution in controversial domestic policies (e.g., Miroff 1976) may be mistaken. Not surprisingly, Ford took the lowest percentage of positions in this issue area, but Clinton's ranking as the next lowest is a surprise. Finally, Eisenhower averaged far more positions than any president on *constituent* policies (again, often foreign policy oriented), while Clinton gave this issue area, by far, the least attention among contemporary presidents. An example is his opposition to Republican efforts to limit military intervention in Bosnia in 1995.

Table 4.4 on selected years is the final comparison in this section. Large differences appear in distributive policy, where positions are taken most often on average during the first year in office. Because they are often not very controversial (see chap. 5), presidents may support such policies to curry favor with Congress and to extend their honeymoon. Regulatory policies are more controversial and, therefore, are offered relatively more often during the last year in office when presidents are lame ducks. Surprisingly, redistributive policies show the least mean variation across selected years in office. Indeed, they are nearly randomly distributed and, since so much legislation occurs in this issue area, presidential positions on them appear not to be made with particular year considerations in mind. Constituent matters are emphasized relatively much more frequently in reelection years, nearly three times more often on average than during presidents' last years.

Position Taking on All Legislation

Overall

Table 4.5 displays overall presidential position taking on all House roll call votes as well as position taking as a percentage of all House votes cast.

Obviously, only House support of such positions is used in chapter 6. Beginning with the first column, it can be seen that presidents on average take about 85 positions on all House votes per year. Clinton took 133 positions in 1995. As expected, Democratic presidents take them far more frequently per year on average (94.1) than do Republicans (76.0). Also, it appears that position taking generally has increased in time across the nine contemporary presidents, certainly since Ford. Finally, presidents average many more positions during their last year, and especially in reelection years, than they do during their first year in office.

Table 4.5 also provides an interesting comparison of position taking as a percentage of House roll call votes. This control is useful because of the increase in roll call voting during the reforms in the House during the 1970s. Overall, presidents take positions on about 31 percent of roll call votes, less than half as often as on important roll call votes. However, the gap between the parties is less in position taking as a percentage of roll calls than for overall position taking. Part of the party difference in overall frequency is probably due to the fact that Republicans were more likely than Democrats to be presidents during the more recent period; thus they had to contend with

TABLE 4.5. Presidential Position Taking on All House Roll Call Votes

	$\bar{x}$/Year Overall Frequency	$\bar{x}$ Percent of All Roll Call Votes
Overall	84.6	30.9
By Party		
Republican	76.0	26.1
Democrat	94.1	37.5
By President		
Eisenhower	49.2	52.9
Kennedy	65.4	55.2
Johnson	98.6	49.8
Nixon	73.5	22.7
Ford	46.0	11.8
Carter	111.9	19.2
Reagan	89.3	22.5
Bush	102.6	22.3
Clinton	90.0	17.0
By Year in Term		
First	65.8	25.9
Last	82.0	37.2
Reelection	83.2	19.5
Other	95.2	33.4

Source: Ragsdale 1996 (table 8.4).

more roll call votes than the three presidents prior to Nixon. Note that position taking as a percentage of total votes does decrease dramatically beginning with Nixon. Indeed, in the more recent period, Republicans average a higher percentage of position taking than do Democrats (see second column of table 4.5). In other words, Carter and, especially Clinton, took a lower percentage of positions on all House roll call votes than did Reagan or Bush.

In short, the seeming increase in overall position taking over time amounts to an actual decrease in position taking as a proportion of all House roll call votes. Among modern presidents, Kennedy took the most positions as a percentage of all votes taken in the House, and Ford, by far, took the fewest. Again, beginning with Nixon, no president took positions on as many as 23 percent of House votes. Presidents take a higher percentage of positions in their last year, nearly twice the rate as in reelection years. As interesting as these overall findings are, considerable variation occurs when examining position taking by political time across policy areas.

Two Presidencies

Overall, it may be seen in table 4.6 that a much greater percentage of presidential position taking occurs in foreign (68.1 percent) than in domestic policy (31.9 percent), perhaps because a larger number of routine matters appear in the latter area. Surprisingly, party differences are not very large, but Republican presidents, as expected, take positions on a slightly greater percentage of foreign House roll call votes than do Democratic presidents. However, the differences between the two parties are not as large as anticipated.

Table 4.6 reveals the much greater variation in position taking by individual presidents that is masked when comparing them by political party. Carter and Reagan, especially, took the highest percentages of positions on foreign policy votes compared to the other presidents, and Ford took the fewest (21.7 percent). Not surprisingly then, Ford took the highest average of positions of any president in domestic policy, but other presidents (namely, Johnson and Nixon) also took relatively many positions on domestic votes. Reagan took the fewest positions of any president on domestic votes. Clinton's heavy domestic emphasis during 1995 appears in such issue areas as crime, national parks, senior citizen housing, water pollution, abortion, and school vouchers.

Differences in position taking by the two presidencies are also evident across selected years in presidents' terms in office (see table 4.6). Reelection years reveal by far the greatest position taking in foreign policy, presumably reflecting the need for presidents to appear "presidential" and remind voters and Congress of their leadership role in this issue area. This finding also squares with literature suggesting that presidential emphases shift more to foreign policy across their terms of office. As hypothesized, presidents do take

TABLE 4.6. Presidential Position Taking (by two presidencies)[a]

	Overall (%)	Foreign (%)	Domestic (%)
Overall	100.0	31.9	68.1
	(84.6)	(26.8)	(57.8)
Party			
Republican	100.0	32.4	67.6
	(76.0)	(24.6)	(51.4)
Democrat	99.9[b]	30.8	69.1
	(94.1)	(29.0)	(65.0)
President			
DDE	100.0	26.6	73.4
	(49.2)	(13.1)	(36.1)
JFK	100.0	30.1	69.9
	(65.4)	(19.7)	(45.7)
LBJ	100.0	23.3	76.7
	(98.6)	(23.0)	(75.6)
RMN	100.0	23.5	76.5
	(73.5)	(17.3)	(56.2)
GRF	100.0	21.7	78.3
	(46.0)	(10.0)	(36.0)
JEC	100.0	40.9	59.1
	(111.9)	(45.8)	(66.1)
RWR	100.0	41.5	58.5
	(89.3)	(37.1)	(52.2)
GHWB	100.0	32.0	68.0
	(102.6)	(32.8)	(69.8)
WJC	100.0	27.2	72.8
	(90.0)	(24.5)	(65.5)
Year in term			
First	100.0	28.1	71.9
	(65.8)	(18.5)	(47.3)
Last	100.0	31.7	68.3
	(82.0)	(26.0)	(56.0)
Reelection	100.0	37.2	62.8
	(90.7)	(33.7)	(57.0)
Other	100.0	32.8	67.2
	(89.2)	(29.3)	(59.9)

Source: Ragsdale 1996 (table 8.4).

Note: Figures in parentheses are base *N*s for the expressed percentages.

[a]*N*s represent mean number per year. The *N*s in this and the next table are not whole numbers because they were averaged as number per year and then into policy and time groupings.

[b]Overall percentages may not equal 100 due to rounding.

relatively more domestic positions during their first year in office (71.9) than during any other year designation. This finding lends support to Paul Light's (1982) notion that the president must "move it or lose it." All in all, the two presidencies dichotomy provided useful distinctions (except by party) on presidential position taking on all roll call votes in the House.

King and Ragsdale Typology

Presidential position taking on House roll call votes also varies significantly by the King and Ragsdale issue areas. Table 4.7 reveals that the greatest percentage of positions are taken in government (24.5 percent) and social welfare (22.1 percent) policy and the least in agriculture policy (4.1 percent). Position taking in the other four issue areas are more equally distributed. Party differences are more prevalent in some issue areas (e.g., foreign aid, defense, and government) than in others. As with important legislation votes, almost no partisan differences in average position taking in social welfare occurred; indeed, it is the issue area of greatest partisan agreement (only .03 percent difference). As might be expected, Democrats push foreign aid and government relatively more, while Republicans give greater average attention to defense and agriculture.

Presidential position taking on House roll call votes by individual president also reveals substantial variation. Carter emphasized the foreign *trade* area to a much greater relative extent than did other presidents (14.8 percent versus just 5.3 for Johnson; see table 4.7). The finding of low mean attention by Clinton (5.6 percent) is surprising given the important and controversial NAFTA and GATT votes that occurred early in his administration. Carter also emphasized foreign *aid* at a relatively much greater level (15.2 percent) than did Clinton (3.9 percent). An example of this by the latter is his favoring aid to the former Soviet Union in 1995. Not surprisingly, Reagan focused much greater average position taking on *defense* issues than did Johnson. Presumably, Johnson's emphasis shifted more toward defense during his later than during his earlier years in office. Fights between Clinton and the Republican 104th Congress occurred on defense spending.

No one will be surprised that Johnson took a higher percentage of his vote positions in *social welfare* (29.4 percent) than any other president. However, Carter's taking the fewest average positions in that issue area among contemporary presidents is unexpected. Clinton took, by far, a higher proportion of positions in the *government* sphere than any other president, while Reagan and Eisenhower took the fewest in that area on average. Ford gave relatively greater attention to the *resource* issue area than any president, and the energy crisis during his and Carter's administrations ensured a high percentage of positions for both presidents. Surprisingly, Clinton gave least

TABLE 4.7. Presidential Position Taking (by King and Ragsdale groupings)[a]

	Overall (%)[b]	TR (%)	AI (%)	DF (%)	SW (%)	GO (%)	RE (%)	AG (%)
Overall	100.0	8.2	9.1	14.5	22.1	24.5	17.5	4.1
	(84.6)	(6.9)	(7.7)	(12.3)	(18.7)	(20.7)	(14.8)	(3.5)
Party								
Republican	100.0	8.3	7.0	17.1	22.2	22.1	18.3	5.0
	(76.0)	(6.3)	(5.3)	(13.0)	(16.9)	(16.8)	(13.9)	(3.8)
Democrat	98.3	6.4	12.0	10.7	21.9	27.8	16.4	3.1
	(94.1)	(7.6)	(11.3)	(10.1)	(20.6)	(26.2)	(15.4)	(2.9)
President								
DDE	99.9	5.7	12.2	8.7	28.0	16.9	19.3	9.1
	(49.2)	(2.8)	(6.0)	(4.3)	(13.8)	(8.3)	(9.5)	(4.5)
JFK	99.9	5.7	14.8	9.6	18.3	30.6	13.3	7.6
	(65.4)	(3.7)	(9.7)	(6.3)	(12.0)	(20.0)	(8.7)	(5.0)
LBJ	100.0	5.3	11.0	7.1	29.4	29.6	14.8	2.8
	(98.6)	(5.2)	(10.8)	(7.0)	(29.0)	(29.2)	(14.6)	(2.8)
RMN	100.1	5.9	6.4	11.3	26.1	29.3	16.7	4.4
	(73.5)	(4.3)	(4.7)	(8.3)	(19.2)	(21.5)	(12.3)	(3.2)
GRF	100.7	7.2	4.0	10.9	18.0	23.3	33.3	4.0
	(46.0)	(3.3)	(1.7)	(5.0)	(8.3)	(10.7)	(15.3)	(1.7)
JEC	100.0	13.2	15.2	12.5	14.7	21.0	21.3	2.1
	(111.9)	(14.8)	(17.0)	(14.0)	(16.5)	(23.5)	(23.8)	(2.3)
RWR	100.1	10.2	5.6	25.8	17.4	17.1	17.5	6.5
	(89.3)	(9.1)	(5.0)	(23.0)	(15.5)	(15.3)	(15.6)	(5.8)
GHWB	100.0	9.1	8.8	14.1	25.3	25.3	15.9	1.5
	(102.6)	(9.3)	(9.0)	(14.5)	(26.0)	(26.0)	(16.3)	(1.5)
WJC	100.1	5.6	3.9	17.8	22.8	37.2	11.7	1.1
	(90.0)	(3.0)	(7.0)	(17.0)	(22.0)	(41.0)	(10.0)	(2.0)
Year in term								
First	100.1	5.5	9.6	13.1	18.5	28.4	19.5	5.5
	(65.8)	(3.6)	(6.3)	(8.6)	(12.2)	(18.7)	(12.8)	(3.6)
Last	100.1	7.0	9.8	15.0	30.5	19.5	14.6	3.7
	(82.0)	(5.7)	(8.0)	(12.3)	(25.0)	(16.0)	(12.0)	(3.0)
Reelection	100.0	11.5	6.5	13.5	20.7	24.0	21.2	2.6
	(83.2)	(9.6)	(5.4)	(11.2)	(17.2)	(20.0)	(17.6)	(2.2)
Other	99.5	8.4	9.3	15.1	22.3	23.9	16.4	4.1
	(89.6)	(7.5)	(8.3)	(13.5)	(20.0)	(21.4)	(14.7)	(3.7)

Source: Position-taking data are from Ragsdale (1996, table 8.6).

Note: Figures in parentheses are base *N*s for the expressed percentages.

[a]For the King and Ragsdale groupings, see legend in table 4.3.

[b]Overall percentages may not equal 100 due to rounding.

average attention to resource policy during his first two years. An example in 1995 is his opposition to Republican efforts to raise highway speed limits. The last issue area is *agriculture,* where it has already been mentioned that the *N*s are small. Eisenhower gave, by far, the greatest mean attention through position taking, and Clinton gave the least. Overall, it is not surprising that agriculture has declined in relative presidential attention based on their positions on House roll call votes.

The final comparison using the King and Ragsdale typology is on the selected year in presidential term of office. It has already been shown that presidents take higher percentages of positions during the last and reelection years than during their first year. Of course, such position taking varies considerably by issue area (see table 4.7). Trade policy indeed is emphasized proportionately much more during the reelection year than during the first year, but such is not the case for foreign aid, where position taking averages much less often during the reelection year. Defense reveals fewer differences, but somewhat more relative positions are taken during the last year. Social welfare policies are emphasized much more frequently during the last than during the first year on average, lending credence to Kennedy's view that taking a stand on such controversial issues as civil rights would diminish support for his other agenda preferences (Miroff 1976). Government issues crop up relatively more often during the first (28.4 percent) than during the last year (19.5 percent). Resources are emphasized more during the reelection year than the last year, while for agriculture mean position taking occurs least often during the presidential reelection year.[6]

Summary and Conclusion

This chapter has presented much data on presidential position taking. It is the only chapter in which actions can be compared directly for votes on important and on all legislation. Overall, more similarities than differences occur, suggesting that (because of their greater significance and fewer numbers to collect) important legislation is a useful alternative to the more cumbersome data on all votes. Of course, using important legislation does reduce the number of votes available for empirical analysis. This is especially true when examining the nine individual presidents and/or the King and Ragsdale categories, where the *N*s in some cells are small.

One of the particular differences between all and important legislation is the much greater frequency of position taking on the latter; twice the rate as on all legislation. Also, important legislation revealed more party variations than did all legislation, especially on foreign policy position taking. Additionally, the number of roll call votes cast relates to the level of presidential position taking. Certainly it occurs *relatively* less frequently in the 1980s and 1990s than during the 1960s.

More specific findings can also be summarized, first by policy areas and then by political time. As expected, position taking overall is greater on domestic than foreign policy, as expected. Of course, Democrats tend to emphasize the former and Republicans the latter. Yet, variations occur within foreign and domestic policy: position taking was greater on defense and resources issues than on foreign aid and agriculture. This finding shows the utility of going beyond the two presidencies dichotomy. Finally, positions are taken relatively most often on redistributive and relatively least on distributive policies.[7] This finding of low position taking on distributive policies is due largely to the addition of the Hinckley foreign policy data, which include no distributive votes.

Useful variations also occurred by the time groupings of data. As expected, Democratic presidents were more assertive than Republican presidents, especially so on votes on important legislation relative to all legislation. Johnson and Kennedy were the most assertive presidents, as anticipated, and Eisenhower and Reagan were the least assertive. This latter finding is not exactly as expected because Ford, who had been so nonassertive in civil rights position taking (Shull 1993), was actually twice as assertive as Reagan in frequency of position taking (but equal on position taking as a percentage of roll call votes). Finally, presidents are more assertive on important legislation during the first and reelection year rather than during the last year, as expected. The pattern changes somewhat on all legislation, where position taking is least during the first year, contrary to expectation. However, when controlling for the number of roll call votes taken, assertiveness is actually least during reelection years, a time when presidents may have less time to devote to more mundane (as opposed to important) legislative matters.

All in all, examining presidential position taking on all aspects of the research, by political time and policy areas, proved a worthwhile enterprise. This is because position taking is not an obligatory action by presidents but, at the same time, has come to be expected by Congress. It does not set the president's agenda but does reveal his policy assertiveness and policy preferences on matters before Congress. Position taking could also reflect ideological distance on the policy agenda. Since position taking is on Congress's agenda, it is an agenda the president cannot control but will seek to influence. As such, position taking should relate considerably to other aspects of presidential-congressional relations, particularly controversy and ultimate support by Congress for these positions. These two concepts, controversy and support, are covered in the book's next two chapters.

CHAPTER 5

Legislative Vote Controversy

with Thomas C. Shaw

Introduction

Conflict (or controversy) is an important concept in the political science literature. Politics generally, and the adoption of public policy specifically, are assumed to result from controversy over allocation of costs and benefits (Kingdon 1984). Many types of political conflict occur, but conflict produced by the interplay of presidential-congressional relations is clearly the most visible at the national level. Although the legal process by definition is confrontational (i.e., prosecution versus defense), only occasionally do such decisions challenge the other two branches of government, especially the presidency. Court decisions themselves seldom have the same appearance of conflict (even though they may be just as political) as that produced by disagreement between the other two branches of the national government.

Some allege that partisan disagreement, particularly divided government, produces gridlock in policy-making (Sundquist 1992; Cutler 1988). Presumably, presidential disagreements with Congress (and within these entities) affect actor relations. This chapter delves into several types of controversy over voting within Congress. Although the controversy examined here is based on roll call votes only, numerous aspects of vote conflict are considered. Indeed, a number of opportunities are available to witness this relationship, and several indicators are presented so that scholars can make their own judgments about applicability. Although this exploration into vote controversy emphasizes Congress, such controversy may influence presidents' other relations with Congress, including position taking, legislative support, and even executive order issuance.

Charles Jones (1995, 11) groups presidential-congressional relations according to the constitutional balance of power. He sees presidential *primacy* only briefly under Johnson (1964–66), *cooperation* early under Eisenhower (1953–55) and Reagan (1981–83) but views the entire remaining post–World War II period as *adversarial*. While Jones stops at the end of the Reagan administration, adversity would likely characterize the Bush administration and the post-1994 period of Clinton's administration. Even Clinton's first two years will be shown here to be quite controversial. Surely Jones's interpretation of presidential-congressional relations is overly strict since much greater variation in controversy occurs in political time.

Obviously, several factors relate to institutional controversy. Contrary to Jones, David Mayhew (1992) and Barbara Hinckley (1994) think relations between presidents and Congress are mostly cooperative rather than conflictual, even during periods of divided government. Certainly split control matters because George Edwards, Andrew Barrett, and Jeffrey Peake (1997) show that much more legislation fails then. Issue area is another important factor in the degree of controversy, for example, Hinckley's suggestion that military intervention is more cooperative than foreign aid. Lance LeLoup and Steven Shull (1993) show that either cooperation or deadlock are possible in all four broad policy areas they considered.

Meaning of Vote Controversy

Controversy in its own right is seldom examined in the scholarly literature on presidential-congressional relations. Rather, most research uses it as an explanatory factor in assessing the president's legislative support or success. Yet, the numerous manifestations of controversy may be important to the relationships themselves and should be explored much more deeply than has occurred heretofore. Most existing research examines controversy as shifting coalitions of legislators. John Bond and Richard Fleisher (1990) examine three types of votes: partisan, bipartisan, and cross-partisan. Research typically compares groupings of like-minded legislators in opposition to other groups with different policy preferences.

Particular attention has been given to political party and/or geographic regional splits. For example, Democrats differ from Republicans, and so measures of party unity should be considered (see, for example, Key 1964; Ripley 1969; Pomper 1980; Patterson and Caldeira 1988). Despite the decline in party identification among voters since the 1970s (Abramowitz 1994; Aldrich 1993), partisan voting in Congress has increased dramatically, especially in the 1990s in the House (see fig. 5.1). This growing partisanship in the "first" branch of government has made the president's role as "chief legislator" more difficult.

In addition, internal and cross-party coalitional alignments (e.g., Northern versus Southern Democrats) or the conservative coalition (Republicans and Southern Democrats aligning against Northern Democrats) may also occur. Indeed, the coalition reached its highest percentage of victories ever in 1995 with 98.2 percent (*CQ Weekly Reports,* January 27, 1996, 195). For-

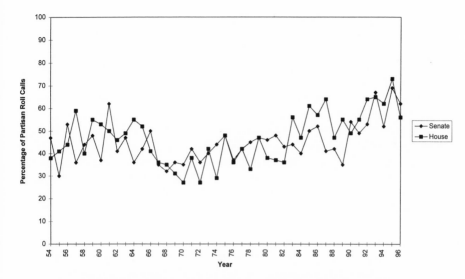

Fig. 5.1. Percentage of partisan roll calls, 1954–96. (Data from *Congressional Quarterly Weekly Report*, January 27, 1996, p. 244.)

tunately for scholars, Congressional Quarterly, Inc. (CQ) has compiled interest group ratings of legislators in several of their annual publications.[1] Most of the literature on legislative support argues that the president's margin of partisans is the most important predictor of support (Bond and Fleisher 1980; Rivers and Rose 1985; Lockerbie and Borrelli 1989; Edwards 1980, 1989).

Literature shows that the ideological preferences of presidents and legislators are closely related to their party identification (Gomez and Shull 1995; Gleiber and Shull 1992; Hayes et al. 1984; Bond and Fleisher 1990). The various indexes of ideology (e.g., Americans for Democratic Action [ADA]) and other group ratings of legislators have long been used in research to determine such policy preferences. Presidential ideology can be ascertained from their position taking on these same roll call votes.[2] Because party and ideological controversies have increased since the 1970s, such cleavages are important elements of conflict. However, since presidential party and ideology are highly correlated,[3] only the former is used here as a control for controversy on important and all legislation.

For important legislation, the specific roll call votes yield considerable amounts of information, such as type of vote (whether voice vote or roll call), vote patterns (both margin of passage and their partisan nature), and number of amendments on each vote.[4] These votes are available for both chambers, so chamber differences in behavior can be monitored. Several authors have urged chamber comparisons, particularly in terms of legislative support of the presidents' vote positions (e.g., Bond and Fleisher 1990; Borelli and Simmons 1992).

With respect to votes on all legislation, the Gary King and Lyn Ragsdale data set is used. The specific indicator is overall in- versus out-party support for presidents' roll call positions (House only) according to their seven issue categories (see also Pomper 1980, 170). Although direct comparisons of controversy between important and all legislation are unavailable, the utility of the measures across the usual groupings of political time and policy areas should allow an assessment of the various measures. More specific operationalizations of the indicators of vote controversy follow:

Operationalization of Controversy

This section discusses the several different measures of controversy over important legislation votes in Congress that are incorporated. Numerous indicators appear from the CQ information about voting their partisan nature, vote passage margins, and whether or not amendments are offered. None of these data appear for our single indicator of controversy on all House roll call votes, but the in- versus out-party support variable does suggest conflict. This indicator reflects the incumbent president's party (in) and the opposition party (out; King and Ragsdale 1988, 51). The latter are already available by the King and Ragsdale groupings and then, of course, further aggregated by the two presidencies.

Important Legislation Votes
Because the votes included are all on final passage of important legislation, controversy probably occurs less on them than on all roll call votes, many of which are amendments. Chamber differences should also occur. However, the two chambers will have about the same frequency of important votes by political time and policy area, so these standard comparisons are not very useful. Nevertheless, chamber differences may appear on several different measures of controversy on votes on the final passage of important legislation.

The average number and proportion of roll calls that are also amendments is another measure of conflict. David Rohde (1994) reveals in an interesting study that amendments do indeed constitute most of the increased number of roll call votes during the 1970s and early 1980s and are, in any event, different from other votes (presumably final passage ones) in Congress. Related research finds amendments differing from all votes across issue areas of public policy (Shull and Klemm 1987). Apart from amendments, the type of vote may also vary, with voice votes suggesting less conflict than recorded votes. Of course, voice votes diminished with congressional reforms in the

1970s. The proportions of voice votes to all votes by political time and policy areas are included.[5]

Other measures of controversy concern the particular margin of passage. First is whether votes are nearly unanimous, sometimes called "hurrah" votes, defined here as greater than a 80 to 20 percent vote margin. Many researchers have urged scholars to separate out such votes in examining legislative support of the president (Edwards 1985, 1989; Bond and Fleisher 1984, 1990; Peterson 1990). This chapter compares hurrah votes to roll call votes on important legislation to ascertain the utility of this distinction. Obviously, a disadvantage of not using all the votes available is that the number of cases is smaller, but the proportion of contested House roll calls by political time and policy areas is easily addressed empirically, and the comparison is a worthwhile enterprise.

The second margin-of-passage variable is mean vote split on each roll call. This conflict measure is operationalized using the following formula:

$$100 \times \left[1.0 - \left(\frac{\text{yeas} - \text{nays}}{\text{yeas} + \text{nays}} \right) \right]$$

Thus, the number of nays is subtracted from the number of yeas and divided by the total number voting on each roll call. Subtracting this value from 1.0 means that the higher the number, the greater the mean vote split (controversy). As with the other variables, an average degree of controversy among votes per year is then derived and subsequently further aggregated by the time and policy groupings.

The final dimension of voting conflict that occurs on these roll calls on important legislation is partisanship, and the proportion of votes when the majority of one party votes against the majority of the other party is examined. A party vote, then, exists if 50 percent or more of Democrats vote against 50 percent or more of Republicans. Although other margins are sometimes used, this is the most common one and is the basis for CQ's data shown in figure 5.1. Another reason for this lower threshold is that since all these votes passed important legislation we want to observe sufficient partisanship from them. Thus, each vote is coded a yes if partisan and no if not, with the higher proportion of partisan votes indicating greater controversy.

All Votes

Although all roll call votes are available in machine-readable form through the University of Michigan's Inter-University Consortium for Political and Social Research (ICPSR), the interest here is on a single variable because that is the only controversy indicator categorized by the King and Ragsdale typology. It is in- (incumbent president's party) versus out-party support of presidents' positions on roll call votes in the House of Representatives. Regrettably, Lyn

Ragsdale provides only percentages in her 1996 update, so no Ns can be reported for controversy on all House roll call votes (see a discussion of this problem in chap. 6).

Ragsdale does not give the numerator (frequency of times Congress votes with the president's position) needed to calculate party support more accurately. Although CQ provides such a numerator, Ragsdale fails to include it. Accordingly, when aggregating the seven policy areas, either into the two presidencies dichotomy or by the political time groupings, means of means are used, which introduces some distortion in the resulting percentages of support on all House roll call votes.

Ragsdale's data show some of the confusion that can occur in trying to differentiate support and success. At one time, CQ called the Boxscore the measure of success but more recently has been using that term to refer to the percentage of presidents' positions that are upheld by Congress. That indicator is sometimes called support, but support now is reserved by CQ to refer to the average membership (the House only in this case) siding with the president's vote positions. Chapter 6 delves into these variables in greater detail.

Expectations for Controversy

Some chamber differences are expected on votes on important legislation. Recall that only votes on final passage of such legislation are included, so essentially roll calls in both chambers appear with about the same frequency by groupings of policy areas and years. However, the chambers may vary across the measures of controversy. The expectation is for more amendments since the 1970s per vote and more in the Senate than in the House. The latter expectation is because of the greater opportunity for amendments due to the structure of the rules in the upper chamber. Also, party voting is expected to be greater in the House than in the Senate, especially in recent years (see fig. 5.1). Related to this expectation is the greater expected contested nature of House votes. Thus, except for the greater proportion of amendments in the Senate, where their introduction is easier, greater controversy on vote splitting should occur in the House.

The amount of controversy (type vote, number of amendments, vote conflict, and partisanship) appearing on these votes should provide useful benchmarks of presidential interactions with Congress, therein determining their respective roles in policy adoption. Although votes on all and important legislation are compared indirectly, less controversy is expected regarding the latter because much of the conflict has been resolved earlier. In other words, votes on important legislation are all on final passage. That is one reason appropriations votes often are not contested. The several types of conflict available offer greater detail on differing aspects of controversy in executive-legislative relations than has appeared heretofore.

Major enactments therefore should be less controversial than is all legislation. King clearly finds greater controversy on key votes (which, presumably, are more often on important legislation) than on all votes (1986). Many votes (including amendments) appearing on an issue probably indicate greater controversy, as do more nonunanimous and voice votes. The five indicators should differentiate chambers, and 1995–96 saw Senate rejection of House-passed constitutional amendments requiring a balanced budget and barring desecration of the flag. Indeed, the Senate softened much of the Republican Contract with America (*CQ Weekly Reports,* January 9, 1996, 119).

Controversy in Congress should vary by the various aggregations of years: by presidential party, by individual president, and by the selected year in presidential term. First, controversy should be greater when Republicans are presidents and less when Democrats occupy the White House. Among individual presidents, conflict should be greater for Ford and Reagan but less for Kennedy and Johnson. Unusually high success appears for Clinton's first two years, but the third and fourth years (with Republicans in control of both chambers) proved much more contentious (see chap. 6). For example, 1995 set records for partisan voting in both chambers of Congress since the beginning of the century (*CQ Weekly Reports,* January 27, 1996, 195) but it was reduced somewhat in 1996. Controversy should be least in a president's first (honeymoon) year and greatest during the reelection and last (lame-duck) years.

All three policy areas (two substantive and one functional) are compared on controversy of important legislation. Foreign policy traditionally has been considered bipartisan but probably is much more partisan than it once was, as the literature has observed (Clausen 1973; LeLoup and Shull 1979b; Holsti and Roseneau 1984). Although voice votes have diminished since the 1970s, they presumably have continued more often on less controversial foreign policy than for domestic policy both before and since. As indicated earlier, in Congress distributive and constituent policies (e.g., agriculture, resources, defense) traditionally have been least contentious and redistributive and regulatory (e.g., social welfare, foreign aid, government) policies most contested (Shull 1983; Peterson 1990).

Results for Important Legislation

This section begins with the presentation in table 5.1 of chamber differences in vote controversy on important legislation. However, the chapter will spend more time attempting to grapple with the several, quite disparate indicators of legislative vote controversy on important legislation. The results of the analysis provided in tables 5.2 and 5.3 reveal some interesting differences and similarities among the numerous indicators of controversy on votes on important legislation by political time and policy area groupings. Findings using voice votes and unanimous votes seem more in line with expectations, while those for mean vote split, amendments, and the partisan nature of votes seem most at variance with expectations.

By Chamber

Table 5.1 illustrates chamber differences in the incorporated indicators of controversy on important legislation. Obviously, about the same number of roll call votes occurs in each chamber. As expected, relatively more voice votes occur in the Senate (thus less controversy), due partly to its less restrictive rules. Also, nearly twice as many amendments occur in the upper chamber for much the same reason. At the same time, the Senate is less partisan than the House, with only about half the rate of partisan votes on final passage of important legislation. In addition, less controversy occurs in the Senate in terms of percentage of nonunanimous votes and vote splitting by 11 percentage points. As stated earlier, these interesting chamber differences on the

TABLE 5.1.   Chamber Differences in Important Legislation (by several indicators of controversy)

	House		Senate	
	N	$\overline{X}$/percent	N	$\overline{X}$/percent
Total votes[a]	312	100.0	305	100.0
Amendments[b]	2,269	7.4	4,248	13.9
Party votes[c]	98	31.4	47	15.4
Mean vote split[d]	312	45.5	305	34.5
Nonunanimous votes[e]	174	55.8	131	43.0
Nonvoice votes[f]	255	81.7	224	73.4

Source: Tables 5.1–5.3 were compiled by authors from CQ information for each important legislation roll call vote.

Note: In all instances, the higher number reflects greater controversy.

[a]Total number of roll call votes and percentage of chamber total.

[b]Total number of amendments and average number per vote.

[c]Number and percentage of roll call votes where 50 percent or more of Democrats opposed 50 percent or more Republicans.

[d]Average of yeas minus nays divided by yeas plus nays subtracted from 1.0.

[e]Number and percentage of roll call votes that were contested (e.g., closer than 80-20 percent split is nonunanimous).

[f]Number and percentage of all non–voice votes (no. non–voice divided by no. roll calls).

indicators of controversy reveal no such variation when grouped by political time or policy areas and, thus, chamber differences are dropped in the subsequent analysis.

Controversy by Political Time

Overall it may be seen in table 5.2 that nearly 78 percent of roll call votes on final passage of important legislation were non–voice votes (hence more controversial on this indicator). Also, about half of roll calls on important legislation are unanimous or nearly so. Nearly eleven amendments are offered on average per vote on important legislation and less than one-quarter of votes on important legislation involve partisan splitting. Now the discussion compares these five controversy variables overall to the political time and policy area aggregations.

Contrary to expectation, lower mean vote splitting occurs under Republican than under Democratic presidents. That is, votes on important legislation are 7.5 percentage points less controversial under the former than the latter on the mean vote split measure. Similarly, controversy, as measured by the percentage of partisan votes, is more than twice as great under Democratic

TABLE 5.2. Average Percentage Controversy on Important Legislation Votes (by political time)

	Non-Voice	Nonunanimous	Vote Split	Partisan	Amendments
Overall	77.6	49.4	40.1	23.5	10.6
By Party					
Republican	82.0	44.0	37.0	15.6	10.5
Democrat	71.3	57.4	44.5	35.1	10.8
By President					
Eisenhower	66.7	58.3	40.9	2.1	9.6
Kennedy	54.8	57.1	42.4	28.6	10.8
Johnson	62.8	50.0	39.4	28.7	12.1
Nixon	86.0	26.4	27.1	6.6	11.8
Ford	89.8	53.1	45.0	28.6	10.2
Carter	91.6	57.8	45.4	34.9	11.3
Reagan	76.2	54.5	43.8	25.7	12.0
Bush	81.3	41.7	35.4	16.7	5.8
Clinton	80.6	80.6	61.5	64.5	5.5
By Year in Term					
First	78.0	62.4	50.5	41.1	11.6
Last	84.3	48.2	36.1	15.7	11.5
Reelection	75.4	47.8	38.2	17.4	9.9
Other	76.2	44.4	37.0	19.1	10.1

Source: See table 5.1.

than Republican presidents. Perhaps Republican legislators increase their party cohesion under Democratic presidents. In addition, nonunanimous (more contested) votes are greater under Democratic presidents (e.g., Republicans under Clinton). As expected, a far higher percentage of non–voice (more controversial) votes appear under Republican presidents. Presumably, this reflects partisan majorities in Congress for Democratic presidents. The number of amendments is about the same regardless of whether a Democrat or Republican is president.

Observed variations in controversy among individual presidents are also unexpected, where the least mean vote splitting appears under Nixon and the most under Clinton. Wide variation by president occurred in the proportion of final passage votes on important legislation that were partisan in nature, with the fewest under Eisenhower and the most, by far, under Clinton. Could this finding have signaled the soon to be emerging Republican majorities that captured both chambers in the 1994 election despite Clinton's relatively high legislative support at that time? Nonunanimous votes were greatest under Clinton and least under Nixon. As expected, non–voice voting indicates 35 percentage points' greater controversy under Ford than Kennedy. At the same time, Clinton also saw the fewest average number of amendments during his first two years, while Reagan (as expected)[6] and Johnson (contrary to expectation) experienced the largest percentages. These findings for the latter variable are somewhat anomalous but do reveal greater relative amendment frequency during the middle years of the study when the number of roll call votes overall were greater.

Some differences by the selected year in presidential term of office also warrant attention. Votes during presidents' first (honeymoon) year were much more contested than during the reelection (by 12.3 percentage points) or last year (by 14.5 percentage points). This may reflect presidents' pushing tougher issues during their first year (Light 1982; Shull 1983). The first year also had a far higher percentage of nonunanimous and partisan roll calls compared to any other year grouping. Less difference in controversy among the four selected years occurred for the average number of amendments per vote or the proportion of non–voice votes. However, controversy on both indicators was greater during the reelection year compared to the first and last year in presidential term.

Controversy by Policy Areas

The measures of controversy show considerable variation in important legislation according to the three policy typologies, again using the overall figures as reference points. First is the two presidencies thesis, which continues to reveal differences on most controversy indicators even though it is a presumably crude dichotomy. Nearly 10 percentage points less vote splitting in domestic than in foreign policy occurs on final passage of important legislation (see table 5.3). Also, foreign votes are more contested than domestic based on the proportion that were nonunanimous. These findings are not congruent with expectations. However, as anticipated, greater controversy in the forms of larger proportion of amendments (by 4 percentage points) and non–voice votes (by 17 percentage points) occurs in domestic policy. At the same time, no difference appears between these two issue areas in the proportion of votes that are partisan. Thus, the findings for the five indicators of important legislation controversy show considerable contentiousness in both the domestic and foreign policy realms.

Controversy according to King and Ragsdale groupings is also mixed. First, mean vote split is clustered fairly closely, with agriculture and foreign aid (as expected) being the most controversial. Resources turned out to be the least contested issue area on that variable and in terms of nonunanimous votes and percentage of partisan votes. Trade and agriculture were by far the most partisan. Foreign aid, not surprisingly, had the greatest percentage of non-unanimous votes. Trade and defense had the smallest proportions of amendments, and resources and agriculture had the most. The three foreign issue

TABLE 5.3.   Average Percentage Controversy on Important Legislation Votes (by policy areas)

	Non-Voice (%)	Nonunanimous (%)	Vote Split (%)	Partisan (%)	Amendments (%)
Overall	77.6	49.4	40.1	23.5	10.6
Two Presidencies					
Foreign	67.8	58.4	45.7	23.6	8.3
Domestic	84.7	42.9	36.0	23.4	12.3
King and Ragsdale					
Trade	73.2	56.1	45.1	34.1	7.9
Aid	67.8	71.1	52.2	25.6	9.5
Defense	66.1	50.4	41.4	18.9	7.8
Social Welfare	86.0	50.0	40.1	29.0	10.1
Government	84.6	44.2	36.5	22.1	15.1
Resources	81.5	32.2	29.8	17.7	11.7
Agriculture	96.0	64.0	50.1	36.0	11.9
Lowi					
Distributive	80.8	62.8	50.1	34.6	11.0
Regulatory	80.0	28.7	27.5	18.0	9.5
Redistributive	81.5	57.3	44.3	26.9	12.7
Constituent	68.5	51.6	41.2	18.6	8.6

Source: See table 5.1.

areas all had considerably less controversy (more voice voting) than any of the four domestic areas in the King and Ragsdale typology. Contrary to expectations, social welfare was about in the middle on these five measures of controversy, indicating that voting on important legislation in this issue area was less contested than expected.

Finally, controversy on important legislation varies according to the Lowi typology. With respect to the percentage of non–voice votes, however, only constituent policy was far from the mean and least contested. On mean vote split, distributive policy is the most and regulatory policy the least controversial. Regulatory policy also had the lowest proportion of partisan votes, the fewest nonunanimous votes, and the fewest amendments attached to its roll call votes among the selected years. Surprisingly, distributive policy was also most, not least, controversial in terms of percentage of partisan and nonunanimous votes. Redistributive policy was fairly controversial, especially with respect to the average number of amendments on important votes.

Results for All Legislation

King and Ragsdale (1988) do not identify the thousands of individual roll call votes on all legislation by policy areas. Therefore, none of the wide variation in support observed for the important legislation discussed earlier is readily available to examine degree of controversy on all votes. Accordingly, levels of in-versus out-party House member support for presidents' vote positions by issue area are used. This variable is a breakdown of the overall support levels used in the next chapter, but observed party differences allow a measure of vote controversy on all roll calls.

Controversy Overall

Average in- versus out-party support for presidents' vote positions in the House appear in table 5.4 for year groupings and table 5.5 for the policy aggregations. Recall that since these two tables are based on means of means some distortion may occur in aggregating these data. Differences in the two means are also reported in both tables. It is evident in both tables that presidents are always supported more by their own (in) party than by the opposition (out) party, with an overall party difference in support of around 30 percentage points.

Controversy by Political Time

Table 5.4 shows somewhat greater party differences by year aggregations than does table 5.5 by policy groupings. Table 5.4 reveals Democrats are supported

TABLE 5.4.   Average In- Versus Out-Party House Member Support for Presidents' Vote Positions (by political time)

	In-Party Support (%)	Out-Party Support (%)	Difference (%)
Overall	71.1	40.1	30.0
By Party			
Republican	67.4	39.8	27.6
Democrat	77.5	40.4	37.1
By President			
Eisenhower	69.1	46.3	22.8
Kennedy	87.3	32.9	50.8
Johnson	80.5	42.6	37.9
Nixon	69.8	51.7	18.1
Ford	70.2	39.9	30.3
Carter	70.3	38.9	31.4
Reagan	64.4	31.3	33.1
Bush	67.1	32.6	34.5
Clinton	74.8	49.3	25.5
By Year in Term			
First	71.1	40.2	30.9
Last	70.3	41.8	28.5
Re-election	71.8	41.6	30.2
Other	71.2	39.4	31.8

Source: Ragsdale 1996, table 8.11.

TABLE 5.5.   Average In- Versus Out-Party House Member Support for Presidents' Vote Positions (by policy areas)

	In-Party Support	Out-Party Support	Difference
Overall	71.1	44.9[a]	25.9
Two Presidencies			
Foreign	72.3	48.2	24.1
Domestic	70.2	42.5	27.7
King and Ragsdale			
Trade	73.1	52.2	20.9
Aid	68.3	45.8	22.5
Defense	75.4	46.3	22.5
Social Welfare	69.1	40.8	28.3
Government	71.5	38.9	32.6
Resources	68.3	47.0	21.3
Agriculture	72.5	43.0	29.5

Source: Ragsdale 1996, table 8.12.

[a]Note that the overall out-party support for policy areas diverges from the value for year aggregations due to distortion when aggregating means of means.

over 10 percentage points more by their party than are Republican presidents, but virtually no difference in out-party support by presidential party appears. Democratic presidents actually obtained slightly more out-party support than did Republicans. Thus, the overall difference in in- versus out-party support clearly favors the Democratic presidents. Individual president variations are considerable. Johnson, and especially Kennedy, were supported by the in party over 80 percent of the time, but Reagan was supported least often (64.4 percent). Reagan was also supported least of any president by the out party. Surprisingly, Nixon received higher overall support from the out party than any modern president. Overall, then, much more party splitting occurred under Kennedy (50.8 percent difference between in- versus out-party support), and the least occurred under Nixon (just 18.1 percent). As useful as party and individual presidents are in differentiating in- versus out-party support of presidents' vote positions, year-in-term shows minimal differences by party in the House. By very narrow margins, presidents are supported least by the in party during the last year but most by the out party then. None of the differences between in- versus out-party support of presidents' vote positions by selected year are dramatic.

Controversy by Policy Areas

As mentioned earlier, for in- versus out-party support, political time groupings are more discerning than are the two substantive policy aggregations presented in table 5.5. Overall, differences in party support are less than for selected year aggregations. Also, no differences in incumbents' party support appear in foreign or domestic policy, but the out party in the House does support presidents' vote positions at higher levels in foreign than in domestic policy, as expected. Visible in table 5.5 are the smaller differences in party support for the King and Ragsdale typology than for individual presidents. Indeed, only 7.1 percentage points separate the greatest in-party support area (defense) over the areas of lowest in-party support (aid and resources). Again, greater differences emerge in out-party support for presidents' vote positions. Table 5.5 shows that trade is supported the most by the out party (the only issue area to exceed 50 percent support), while government is supported the least. The least difference in incumbent presidential versus opposition party support occurs for trade while the greatest difference occurs in the government issue area.

Summary and Conclusion

This chapter has examined several aspects of vote controversy on important and all legislation. The comparisons began with chamber differences on important legislation, and substantial differences emerged. Presumably due to institutional factors, such as rules, many more non–voice votes and amendments (indicating greater controversy) occurred in the Senate than in the House. However, the Senate showed less mean vote splitting and partisan vote divergence on votes on final passage of important legislation. This finding squares with CQ's reporting that although partisan voting has increased in both chambers since the early 1970s generally it has been lower in the Senate than in the House since the 1980s.

Because all the important legislation passed Congress, such votes were not as controversial as were all roll call votes. Thus, important legislation votes are on the low side of mean vote splitting; they seem to generate many amendments, but just 25 percent of final passage votes involve split party voting. Perhaps surprisingly, such vote splitting occurs less frequently when Republicans rather than Democrats are presidents. Also, a higher proportion of votes are partisan under Democratic presidents. Presumably, this finding reflects that Republicans are more willing than Democratic members of Congress to challenge a president of the opposite party.

When examining individual presidents, least controversy in vote splitting occurred under Nixon and most appeared under Clinton. The latter's prospects worsened even more during 1995–96. Also, Clinton had, by far, the greatest percentage of nonunanimous and partisan votes during 1993–94. However, fewer amendments were observed under Clinton than for any other president. Not surprisingly, Johnson had a large proportion of voice voting (low controversy) but, unexpectedly, also had a large proportion of amendments on final passage of important legislation. Year-in-presidential-term revealed more vote splitting and more partisan voting during honeymoon years. Amendments were more prevalent during reelection years.

As expected, much more controversy occurred in domestic than in foreign policy as measured by the number of amendments and non-voice votes. Ironically, however, foreign policy votes were more contested in that they had greater vote splitting and more nonunanimous votes. Again, when looking at the King and Ragsdale categorization, the numerous indicators of controversy on important legislation worked differently. The three foreign issue areas were just as contested as the four domestic ones. On the other hand, social welfare was not nearly as contested as were other King and Ragsdale issue areas, like foreign aid and agriculture. The Lowi typology also revealed useful differences in controversy regarding votes on important legislation. Findings frequently were surprising, with distributive policies usually more controversial than regulatory ones.

The analysis then shifted to the single indicator of controversy on all legislation, the in- versus out-party percentage of House support for presidents' vote positions. Overall, their own (in) party supported presidents about

30 percentage points more than the opposition party. Democratic presidents are supported much more often by members of the in party than are Republicans. However, no difference occurred in out-party support for Democratic versus Republican presidents. Not surprisingly, Kennedy and Johnson were supported most by the in party and Reagan supported least. Yet Reagan also was supported least by the opposition party, while Nixon, surprisingly, received the greatest out-party support of any president. Perhaps this is due to the liberal nature of many Nixon domestic policies (Ripley 1972) and the seeming "internationalism" (as opposed to isolationism) of his foreign policies. Year-in-presidential-term did little to differentiate in- versus out-party House member support for presidents' vote positions.

The two substantive typologies were less useful than political time in comparing in- versus out-party support for presidents' vote positions in the House. Virtually all differences were fewer for the latter than for the former. For example, no difference in party support for presidents' foreign policy positions emerged, but the out party does support presidents more in that issue area as the two presidencies literature suggests. The King and Ragsdale categorization is not very discriminating in tapping support by party. Just seven percentage points differentiate the seven issue areas in incumbent party support, although greater variation occurs in opposition party support. Out-party support exceeds 50 percent only in trade, while presidential vote positions in the government area are supported least often on average by the out party in the House.[7]

The findings in this chapter on the controversy surrounding voting decisions in Congress on both important and all legislation have been varied but also provocative. Many indicators have been used for the former, but, as has been the practice throughout this volume, they are provided to allow readers to ascertain their relative utility. Which indicator one uses should depend upon the specific research question being considered.[8] The wealth of data provided by individual votes on the final passage of important legislation is not as easily gathered for all legislation. Such would be a monstrous data set indeed. However, suggestions will appear in the concluding chapter regarding the relative utility of these indicators.

Controversy within Congress on roll call voting has many facets and, therefore, should be considered multidimensional (Uslaner 1993). While one might think that internal legislative conflict has little relationship to the presidency, the primary argument in this book is that the executive and legislative environments are inextricably related. Even seemingly internal aspects like voting in Congress takes place in a broader political environment. Controversy should relate to presidential legislative support (chap. 6) and even to executive order issuance (chap. 7). Chapter 8 suggests how research on controversy and on other aspects of presidential-congressional relations may be furthered.

CHAPTER 6

Legislative Support

Presidential-congressional relations have been observed empirically for over 40 years through measurements of presidents' legislative success or support, from indicators collected by Congressional Quarterly, Inc (CQ). Virtually no attention has been given to the other components of presidential-congressional relations used in this book: presidential position taking on legislative votes, controversy on such votes, or executive order issuance within a legislative context. Examining presidents' legislative success began first with Aaron Wildavsky's ([1966] 1991) "two presidencies" thesis. Subsequent scholars adapted different indicators of success and, particularly, support in studying this topic (see selections in Shull 1991). Of course, the two presidencies has not been the only concern of scholars, and some have focused particular attention on determinants of success or support. Using sophisticated modeling and multivariate analyses (e.g., Bond and Fleisher 1990; Peterson 1990), success and support variables have sometimes been used to infer leadership and influence in presidential-congressional relations (Edwards 1980, 1989). Their extensive utilization by scholars has prompted debate about what they actually measure.

This chapter begins with conceptual and measurement questions about executive-legislative relations. It considers concepts identified by CQ: success, support, key votes, and then related ideas used by other authors. CQ has collected both success and support measures for a considerable period of time and, despite problems, they have been widely used in the literature of presidential-congressional relations. Variations on an earlier available success measure continue (Light 1982; Peterson 1990), and this chapter assesses the numerous indicators. The second, shorter section of the chapter provides operationalization and expectations for the incorporated variable, presidents' legislative support. The remainder of the chapter presents findings on the CQ support measure across the two substantive typologies of public policy and the groupings of political time.

Conceptual Issues

Legislative Success

At one time, CQ measured legislative *success* through its boxscore indicator. The organization included in this measurement only the specific legislative requests contained in the president's messages to Congress and other public statements and whether or not Congress enacted such measures within the same calendar year. Although CQ did not specify which statements they used, Shull (1983) and others have included all messages (taken from *Public Papers of the Presidents*) as opposed to just the State of the Union or major speeches used by some scholars (e.g., Light 1982; Cohen 1980). Policies emanating from the executive branch that are endorsed by the president but not specifically requested by him are excluded. When such requests or proposals are substantially changed or amended by Congress, CQ made a judgment (without supplying specific coding rules) about whether the legislation conforms to the president's original request. (For an example of coding rules, see *CQ Almanac* 1963, 86.)

Success is a tangible measure of presidential preferences that provides numerous advantages to scholars (Hammond and Fraser 1984a; Shull 1983; Rivers and Rose 1985; Spitzer 1983; Covington et al. 1995). Unfortunately, the disadvantages of the data are just as pronounced, leading CQ to abandon the box score measure after 1975.[1] Suffice it to say that CQ had made judgments about success with which they no longer felt comfortable. The organization's principal apprehension about its box score seems to be that writers were quoting aggregate figures (of presidential success, for example) without adequately considering the substance of the initiatives themselves or qualitative or other quantitative factors that may influence the results.

Problems associated with the box score have been discussed by many scholars (Bond, Fleisher, and Krutz 1996; Bond and Fleisher 1990; Edwards 1980, 1985, 1989; King and Ragsdale 1988; Peterson 1990; Pritchard 1986; Shull 1983). Its most widely recognized drawbacks include the following: first is an insensitivity to legislation that takes more than one year to pass (Bond and Fleisher 1990; Cohen 1980, 4; Edwards 1980; Peterson 1990; Shull 1983). This is because calendar year is the unit of analysis. Paul Light (1982) and others show that many of the president's legislative requests subsequently are repeated. A second problem is ambiguity in identifying actual legislative proposals by the president (King and Ragsdale 1988; Shull 1983). They are derived from presidents' speeches but sometimes come from other "top officials." Third is the lack of scores for individual legislators (Edwards 1980, 1985, Peterson 1990; Shull 1983), making only aggregate rather than individual legislator analysis possible (Bond, Fleisher, and Krutz 1996). Finally, the equal weighting of all requests (Edwards 1980; Shull 1983) does not distinguish the important from the trivial.[2]

Despite these acknowledged problems, some scholars still consider box scores a potentially valuable database (Spitzer 1983; Hammond and Fraser 1984b; Shull 1983). CQ box scores are far from perfect, but they do provide a conceptually valid measure of presidential success (on *his* preferences) in

Congress. Improvements can be made by modifying the coding rules and expanding the presentation of the data (Shull 1983). Mark Peterson (1990) used a form of the box score in his analysis and rekindled interest in similar measures. His changes in part address some of the empirical problems that led to the demise of the box score indicator of success.[3]

In recent years, CQ has used success in a different way, analogous to what Lyn Ragsdale (1996, 383) calls concurrence. Now success connotes the proportion of presidential vote positions that are upheld by Congress. Thus, it is no longer an indicator of presidents' agenda success but of legislative agreement (both chambers) with his vote positions. The formula for CQ's success score is the number of times Congress upholds presidents' vote positions divided by the number of positions taken per year. Unlike the earlier success measure, CQ's current one is much more closely related to their support score; both now use number of presidential positions as the denominator. The vote is the unit of analysis. A depiction of CQ's current success score (the average number of times the presidents' vote positions prevailed) from 1953 to 1996 appears in figure 6.1.

Legislative Support

The second CQ measure is the *support* score, available overall and for individual legislators, the latter being the unit of analysis. Scholars and journalists alike have relied on this indicator, collected continually since 1957.[4] However, it is not a measure of successful presidential initiatives to Congress (the president's agenda) but rather his response (position taking) to issues before Congress that it upholds or rejects. Therefore, it is Congress's rather than the president's agenda that becomes the focus, and scholars should not confuse the two. With the support measure, similar content analysis judgments of presidential preferences are required, and some margin of error may also exist.

In measuring support, CQ uses all public messages to determine the president's position on roll call votes (see chap. 4). CQ includes procedural votes only if they reflect a substantive issue while votes on appropriations "generally" are not included. Only members who cast a yea or nay are counted in calculating the scores. Thus, scores for individual members may be based on different numbers of roll call votes. As with success, one can calculate a percentage combining House and Senate support for the president. Again, the organization makes judgments as to whether particular votes approximate a president's stated policy preference. (For an example of coding rules, see *Congressional Roll Call* 1986, 23-C.)

Like the original success measure (the box score), the support score possesses both advantages and disadvantages. Because a support score is assigned to each member of Congress, it is possible to construct a variety of

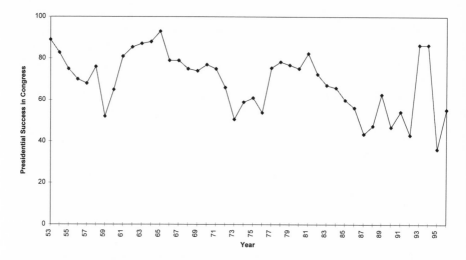

Fig. 6.1. Presidential success in Congress, 1953–96. (Data from _Congressional Quarterly Weekly Reports,_ January 27, 1996, p. 239. Ragsdale [1996] calls this measure congruence, the percentage of times presidents' vote positions prevail.)

data aggregations. For example, these individual scores can be combined by state, region, party, ideology, and so on. As a result, the support score is more versatile than the box score, which is inherently limited by its high level of aggregation. Of course, support scores are a poorer measure of presidential preferences. Critics commonly note three disadvantages: first, as with the box score, all issues are weighted equally (Bond, Fleisher, and Krutz 1996; Bond and Fleisher 1990; Edwards 1980, 1985; Peterson 1990). Second, ambiguities exist in identifying which votes to use (Bond and Fleisher 1990; Edwards 1985). Obviously, such decisions affect the results, and all roll call votes are included here. Finally, some argue that bias is introduced by including routine, noncontroversial votes (Bond and Fleisher 1990; Edwards 1985; Peterson 1990).

Comparing Success, Support, and Key Votes

Students of presidential-congressional relations need to keep in mind the very different nature of CQ's presidential legislative success (both indicators) and legislative support (both indicators). Shull (1983) found that presidents from 1953 to 1975 averaged only 44 percent (old box score) success, but their overall support (CQ's current success measure) from Congress on votes was much higher (73 percent). Why should every president fare better on CQ's support than on its original success score? A proposal by the president must pass both houses to be approved. His position on a roll call, however, often refers to any recorded vote in either chamber. Obviously, since the early 1970s, support is based more on amendments (given the substantial increase in the number of roll call votes documented in chap. 5) than previously. In addition, although final passage of legislation usually constitutes a roll call, many votes are not on final passage.

Shull (1983) observed that support and box score success seem similar but evidenced different patterns (r = .61) and found that presidents' legislative support averaged considerably higher than legislative success (box score).[5] Using key votes, Lee Sigelman ([1979] 1991) observes relatively lower support for presidents on major issues (even quite a bit lower than the success measure). This reveals that key votes are more contentious (and therefore atypical) compared to positions on non-key roll calls. Existing research already focuses too much on unique phenomena, as typified by Sigelman's key votes. The support score offers a broad spectrum of presidential-congressional interactions (more so than the box score [Bond, Fleisher, and Krutz 1996, 110]), encompassing both routine and controversial matters. Ragsdale's (1996) legislative support of presidents' vote positions in the House by issue area is incorporated here.

In order to deal with some of the criticisms of the CQ support score, scholars have offered refinements. George Edwards (1985) presents four alternative indices: overall support, nonunanimous support, single-vote support, and key votes. Gary King and Ragsdale critique Edwards' nonunanimous and single-vote support measures as having "severe selection bias" (1988, 61; see also Achen 1986). Interestingly, Edwards finds that all four of the indices "have a great deal in common," and the differences among them "are typically small" (1985, 683). However, he does caution that significant disparities among the indices need to be considered. In particular, Edwards expresses some concerns about scholars' use of key votes but admits they provide a parsimonious measure (673–74).

Edwards was not the first to consider key votes, a much smaller subset of seemingly important votes than all votes, available since 1945 (see Sigelman [1979] 1991; Shull and LeLoup [1981] 1991). Shull and Jim Vanderleeuw (1987) study key votes by examining CQ's criteria for their identification and inclusion. They examine the three decision rules provided by the organization and find them somewhat ambiguous. They include "a matter of controversy, a test of presidential or political power, and a decision of potentially great impact on the lives of Americans" (1987, 573). The authors conclude that these particular votes are a better measure of presidential power than of controversy in Congress.

Key votes, however, emphasize the controversial over the routine and, thus, are atypical of all roll call votes. Presidents take positions on only about 31 percent of all votes but on virtually all key votes. Others also argue that key votes overrepresent controversial votes (King 1986). Key votes have their uses but, as suggested in chapter 1 in the discussion of the two presidencies, sometimes few observations occur. Accordingly, they suffice for broad analysis but are rarely beneficial for examining votes according to functional or substantive policy areas. Some authors have thought of the CQ indicators as measuring presidential influence in Congress (Edwards 1980), the concept discussed next.

What Does Influence Mean?

Robert Dahl defines this concept as "A influences B to the extent that he gets B to do something that he would otherwise not do" (1963, 40).[6] This definition of influence (or an analogue of it) is widely accepted by members of the scholarly community (Edwards 1991; Mouw and MacKuen 1992; Pritchard 1983; Sullivan 1991b). From this perspective, influence in Congress is observed only when members deviate from the way they would normally vote (Mouw and MacKuen 1992, 581). This more stringent definition undercuts past efforts to explain presidential influence using box scores and support scores (Bond and Fleisher 1980; Edwards 1980). Anita Pritchard argues that "support scores indicate only how often congressional members vote as the president would have liked them to vote, which does not mean the president influenced the voting decision" (1986, 481). Thus, support scores reflect assertiveness and/or policy congruence, not necessarily influence. Fortunately, scholars are beginning to develop more sophisticated techniques for measuring influence.

Calvin Mouw and Michael MacKuen (1992) use an approach that establishes a baseline indicating the ideological orientation of each member of Congress. They argue that influence occurs when the president's action shifts support to undecided members and even opponents. Their procedure compares the predicted vote for members of Congress to their actual vote; switches or changes toward the president's position are counted as influence. In contrast, Pritchard (1983) attempts to measure influence by deriving for individual legislators two types of scaled voting scores in five major policy domains (see Clausen 1973). One score is for "general" votes in a policy area; the other is for the subset of policy votes on which the president took a public stand. The scores are aggregated by party, and a net change is calculated across policy dimensions. Deviations toward the preferences of the president are presumed to result from presidential influence (Pritchard 1983, 693–94).

Both of these approaches use creative measurement strategies of presidential influence and make significant contributions to the body of knowledge. Their findings do infer influence based on changes in expected voting outcomes. Determinations of "normal" or "usual" voting behavior can be subjective. As a result, biases reflected in this standard are, to an extent, transferred to the identification of change in voting decisions. This limitation is mentioned, not as a critique, but as a call for a more refined measure of presidential influence. Surely influence must include the notion of changing legislators' behavior.

Using Other Indicators

Scholars have sought other measurement strategies to develop indicators of presidential-congressional relations. Thomas Hammond and Jane Fraser analyzed success (box score) rather than the key vote support of Mouw and MacKuen by creating baseline models that reflect statistical chance (1984a, 1984b). Each baseline model is designed to embody certain assumptions about the voting behavior of members of Congress, the importance of party, and the existence of factions. The authors concede that they "are trying to judge presidential performances, not explain them" (644). There is no attempt to discern which model best reflects the actual conditions that affect success. As a result, this baseline approach provides interesting results, but it does not directly explain success.

Terry Sullivan offers a measurement strategy that relies on presidential administration head counts used to determine the initial positions of members of Congress. The aggregated difference between initial positions and final votes is Sullivan's approximation of influence, which he calls "sway" (1991b, 693). This strategy is appealing because change is measured directly; it is not based on a subjective construct. Of course, Sullivan's approach is vulnerable to criticism. In particular, Edwards (1991) questions his understanding of influence and the reliability of head counts. Also, head counts are ascertained by the administration itself and may serve political purposes more than methodological ones. In addition, they are available for only a few administrations.

Nevertheless, Sullivan addresses Edwards's concerns, stating that "change is central to the definition of influence" (1991c, 732). Given this perspective, future research on influence should move toward a more direct measure of change. Sullivan is on the right track; conceptually, the change in initial positions and final votes seems like the most appropriate measure of influence. The key obstacle to this approach is in the identification of initial legislator positions and whether such head counts are comparable across administrations; indeed, they are not available for all modern presidencies. Despite these limitations, head counts reduce the president's information and time costs since he has no need to influence a member already in agreement with his position.

Assessment

The previous discussion treats success, support, and influence as three distinct concepts. By observing these distinctions, scholars can more easily clarify what they want to explain. "Although this may appear to be a straightforward or even pedestrian task, it is actually a stage at which researchers may easily stumble and undermine the remainder of their efforts" (Edwards 1989, 16). Although success and support scores have proved useful, scholars should also concentrate on more refined measures. Political time and policy area approaches capture the temporal nature and the dimensions of congressional decision making. Advances in the measurement of success, support, and influence will not be easy; scholars will inevitably face formidable problems and difficulties. However, understanding the measurement controversies better prepares the reader to assess the CQ support score used here as well as other alternatives.

Measurement Concerns

The second section of this chapter lays out the operationalization for legislative support of the president. Overall support divides the denominator of position taking from chapter 4 and then calculates the average percentage support of the presidents' vote positions for the year. Ragsdale provides these data for the House only according to her typology, but problems arise, as will be discussed shortly. Also, she does not provide the policy categorizations for legislative success. Next, the expectations for support are compared for the two presidencies and the King and Ragsdale categorization across political time. To reiterate, support on important legislation is not examined here because the roll call votes used are on final passage bills only.

Measuring Support

The presidents' legislative support reflects the mean percentage of members of the House who vote yea on a measure the president favors or nay on one he opposes. It is not the commonly used individual member support score.[7] Legislative success (both indicators) and support of the president and the conditions that seem to influence them have been examined extensively in the literature. Indeed, considerable, often multivariate, analysis has been conducted using these variables or variations of them (Cohen 1980; Rivers and Rose 1985; Edwards 1989; Bond and Fleisher 1990). The legislative support score is utilized here for all legislation and is the average percentage of the House-only agreement with presidents' positions categorized by Ragsdale (1996). Despite problems with the support score documented earlier, its wide use in the literature necessitates a thorough analysis here.

Regrettably, like the in- versus out-party support score used in chapter 5, Ragsdale provides only a percentage figure; she does not give the numerators (frequency of members voting with the president's position) needed to calculate overall or individual party support more accurately. Although CQ provides such numerators, Ragsdale fails to include them. Accordingly, when aggregating the seven policy areas, either into the two presidencies dichotomy or by political time, means of means are used, which introduces some distortion in the resulting percentages of overall support.[8]

Expectations for Support

Previous literature has shown that presidents generally fare well on support of their vote positions from Congress. Obviously, such support in the House should vary considerably according to groupings of the data by the three time periods and by the two substantive typologies. It should be obvious by now that Democratic presidents should be supported more than Republicans because they have larger numbers of their partisans in Congress, at least within the time frame analyzed. Also, presidents should be supported at higher levels during their first (honeymoon) year in office than during the reelection or last (lame-duck) year.

Certainly, presidents' overall legislative support should be greater in foreign than in domestic policy (see various studies in Shull 1991). Clearly, however, differences should occur within domestic and foreign policy. Presidents probably are supported more in the defense sphere (Rohde 1994) but less so in foreign aid or trade. Within domestic policy, presidents probably receive greater legislative support for distributive policies, like agriculture and resources, than regulatory or redistributive ones, like government or social welfare (Peterson 1990; Shull 1983, 84). Literature suggests presidents are deferred to in foreign policy but not when they take benefits from one group and give them to another (i.e., redistributive policy; Shull 1983). Thus, differences in presidents' legislative support should occur across political time and policy areas.

Results of Analysis

The CQ support score overall and for the two substantive typologies (two presidencies and King and Ragsdale) will now be examined. Recall that support on important legislation vote positions is not considered because that data set includes only measures that pass Congress. Accordingly, presidents are always supported when they take a pro position and always opposed when they take an anti position on major legislation. Therefore, little purpose is served by examining support on final passage of important legislation votes.[9] Because a single dependent variable is incorporated in both this and the next chapter, the data are presented slightly differently and somewhat more comprehensively than in the preceding chapters.

Overall

Overall, presidents are supported an average of 57.4 percent in the House when they take positions on roll call votes.[10] As would be expected, the advantage in overall support favors Democratic presidents by 12.4 percentage points because Democrats always had their partisans in control of the House during the period examined (see table 6.1). Indeed, it is somewhat surprising that the difference in legislative support by presidential party is not even greater, particularly in more recent years when partisan voting and conflict in Congress have increased dramatically (see chap. 5).

Overall support varies considerably when examining the nine individual presidents who served from 1957 to 1994. Not surprisingly, Johnson received the greatest and Reagan received the least support on average for their House vote positions (see table 6.1). Carter did poorly among Democratic presidents

TABLE 6.1. Average Legislative Support for the President in the House of Representatives

	Overall %
Overall	57.4
By Party	
Republican	53.8
Democratic	65.2
By President	
Eisenhower	57.7
Kennedy	66.3
Johnson	69.2
Nixon	61.1
Ford	56.9
Carter	59.7
Reagan	47.7
Bush	48.9
Clinton	62.4
By Year in Term	
First	60.9
Last	55.1
Reelection	54.2
Other	58.6

Source: Data on average percentage agreement in the House of Representatives for presidents' vote positions. They are means of the yearly percentages provided by Ragsdale (1996, table 8.10).

and actually fared worse than Republican Nixon. Ford took relatively few positions (see chap. 4), perhaps accounting for his higher than expected legislative support. Reagan and Bush took relatively more positions than did Ford but received much lower support. Despite Clinton's high success in 1993–94 (see fig. 6.1), his average support was more than 20 percentage points lower.

Finally, differences in overall support are not great across the selected year in presidents' terms, except for the honeymoon (first) year when presidents receive, as expected, greatest average support. By a very narrow margin, they receive least support during the reelection year. These overall differences in support in table 6.1 are disappointing but should be magnified when incorporating year aggregations with policy typologies, which are considered next.

Two Presidencies Thesis

As the two presidencies thesis contends, presidents are indeed supported somewhat more frequently on foreign policy than on domestic issues, but the difference of only 3.9 percentage points (see table 6.2) is too small to be significant. The political party of the president begins to distinguish this relationship, although as others have observed (Bond and Fleisher 1990; Fleisher and Bond [1988] 1991), a two presidencies effect occurs only for Republicans. A mere 1.0 percent differentiates foreign and domestic support for Democrats, but a more identifiable 6.5 percent difference is found for Republican presidents.

Observation of individual presidents, shown in table 6.3, reveals that this lower Republican legislative support particularly appears for our three most recent Republicans (Ford, Reagan, and Bush).[11] Some presidents (e.g., Johnson and Nixon) reveal almost no difference between domestic and foreign legislative support but, for others (e.g., Kennedy and Ford), the differences are pronounced. Carter, Clinton, and, especially, Reagan, were the only presidents to fare worse in foreign policy than in the domestic realm. Carter was widely criticized for his handling of foreign policy, and some observers feel that the

TABLE 6.2. Average Percentage Agreement (Support) in the House (two presidencies; by presidential party)

Party	$\overline{X}$ Overall Percent	Foreign	Domestic
Republican	53.8	57.3	50.8
Democrat	64.9	64.2	65.2
Totals	57.4	59.9	56.0

Source: Ragsdale 1996, table 8.10.

TABLE 6.3.   Average Support in the House (two presidencies;
by president)

President	$\overline{X}$ Overall Percent	Foreign	Domestic
Eisenhower	57.7	62.1	55.9
Kennedy	66.3	70.5	64.3
Johnson	69.2	68.1	69.8
Nixon	61.1	61.6	61.1
Ford	56.9	57.9	47.0
Carter	59.7	57.3	61.2
Reagan	47.7	53.6	42.9
Bush	48.7	51.8	46.3
Clinton	61.3	59.0	62.1
Totals	57.4	59.9	56.0

Source: Ragsdale 1996, table 8.10.

Iran-hostage crisis in late 1980 cost him reelection against Ronald Reagan. Yet Reagan's support on his House roll call vote positions was significantly lower than for any other president in domestic policy and lower than all but Bush in foreign policy.

The selected year in presidents' term of office also reveals the utility of policy designations. Overall, the differences appear minimal, and presidents are somewhat less likely to be supported during the last and reelection year than during the first year, but none of the differences are large. These variations in support in table 6.4 are largely nonexistent in domestic policy, but greater variation appears in foreign policy. As expected, presidents are supported more often in the first (honeymoon) than in the last (lame-duck) year in office. This 8.6-percentage-point difference seems to be important.

TABLE 6.4.   Average Support in the House (two presidencies;
by year in presidential term)

Year in Term	$\overline{X}$ Overall Percent	Foreign	Domestic
First	60.9	63.3	57.5
Last	55.1	54.7	57.5
Reelection	54.2	57.7	55.8
Other	58.6	59.4	57.0
Totals	57.4	59.9	56.0

Source: Data from Ragsdale 1996, table 8.10; calculated by author.

King and Ragsdale Typology

Perhaps not surprising given what has been observed so far, the King and Ragsdale categorization does have greater discriminating power than the two presidencies dichotomy. Overall, trade positions are supported much more often than any of the other six issue areas, thereby accounting for a good bit of the variance between domestic and foreign policy. Recall too that trade is probably more a sector-specific concern than are some other issue areas, making it less prone to partisan conflict and broader legislative support (Gibson 1995). Congress supports presidents the least on three domestic issue areas (social welfare, government, and resources) but not dramatically less than on foreign aid, which at 57.7 percent is just about the average (overall) level of support (see table 6.5).

Party differences are more insightful for the King and Ragsdale typology than they are for the two presidencies because now Democrats reveal almost as much range in support (61 percent for foreign aid to 70 percent for foreign trade) as do Republicans (48 percent for social welfare to 58 percent for foreign trade). Nearly a 21-percentage-point gap between the parties exists in social welfare, whereas the smallest gap in support (4.7 percentage points) exists in foreign aid. Foreign aid, then, is not nearly as partisan as expected in legislative support of the president.

Variations in support by individual presidents are substantial across the King and Ragsdale substantive issue areas. More than 21 percentage points separate Johnson and Reagan in overall support (see table 6.6). Again, as a rule, Democratic presidents did much better than Republicans. The one exception was Carter who scored just above the mean in overall support and, surprisingly, Clinton whose overall support was only slightly better than Nixon's. The greatest level of support given any president was Kennedy on defense policy (nearly 80 percent) and the least was given Ford on social welfare (less than 38 percent). However, Reagan fared considerably worse than Ford except on social welfare and, especially, defense.[12] Only in agricul-

TABLE 6.5. Average Support in the House (King and Ragsdale; by presidential party)

Party	X̄ Overall %	TR	AI	DF	SW	GO	RE	AG
Republican	53.8	58.3	56.0	55.4	47.9	51.8	49.8	56.9
Democrat	64.9	70.0	60.7	65.4	68.4	61.9	67.9	61.9
Totals	57.4	62.5	57.7	59.1	55.4	55.5	56.5	58.8

Source: Ragsdale 1996, table 8.10.
Note: See legend in table 4.3.

ture, where chapter 4 revealed that few positions occur, did Reagan reach the mean level of presidential support in one of the seven issue areas. Eisenhower obtained the greatest range in support (at 28 percentage points), while Johnson's support was more even (a 15-percentage-point spread). Foreign aid was, by far, the issue area with the least range in support (15 percent variation) among the nine contemporary presidents. A range in support of approximately 35 percent occurred for individual presidents in four of the King and Ragsdale categories—two foreign and two domestic—(trade, defense, social welfare, and resources).

Recall that variations in presidents' legislative support are not great by the selected year in their terms of office. On all policy areas but foreign aid and agriculture, presidents obtained greater support in their honeymoon year than in their lame-duck year. By far, the highest level of support was in agriculture during the last year (80.2 percent), but recall that few observations occur then. Similarly, the lowest support was also in the last year in defense (43.6 percent) and government (41.6 percent; see table 6.7). Accordingly, the range in support was far greater—more than twice as many percentage points—in the last year (36 percentage points) than in any other year. Also, it is clear that two of the domestic issue areas, agriculture at 25 percentage points and resources at just 5 percentage points, show the greatest ranges in support by the selected year in office. The range in support of only about six percentage points for "other" year provides empirical support for the contention that they are random and devoid of any theoretical or empirical utility.

TABLE 6.6.   Average Support in the House (King and Ragsdale; by presidential party)

Pres.	$\overline{X}$ Overall	TR	AI	DF	SW	GO	RE	AG
DDE	57.7	73.9	60.8	45.2	57.7	56.0	52.0	56.8
JFK	66.3	75.2	62.6	79.8	74.6	62.8	58.6	54.8
LBJ	69.2	71.6	66.4	65.6	65.4	65.3	76.3	60.6
RMN	61.1	69.2	59.9	63.4	56.3	65.5	61.8	49.6
GRF	56.9	61.2	61.0	54.6	37.8	46.0	50.7	57.2
JEC	59.7	61.0	51.7	59.1	64.5	59.5	59.5	70.8
RWR	47.7	48.8	50.8	55.2	39.9	42.2	43.9	57.8
GHWB	48.9	44.3	52.0	54.3	46.5	48.9	41.2	65.1
WJC	62.4	67.4	62.2	55.9	62.9	56.6	77.0	a
Totals	57.4	62.5	57.7	59.1	55.4	55.5	56.5	58.8

Source: Ragsdale 1996, table 8.10.

Note: See legend in table 4.3.

a Although Ragsdale (1996, table 8.6) credits Clinton as taking two agriculture positions, she treats his support in that issue area as missing (table 8.10) as if he took no positions.

TABLE 6.7. Average Support in the House (King and Ragsdale; by year in presidential term)

Year	X̄ Overall	TR	AI	DF	SW	GO	RE	AG
First	60.9	70.5	56.5	62.2	59.1	58.0	58.0	55.2
Last	55.1	54.7	65.4	43.6	53.5	41.6	53.9	80.2
Reelection	54.2	58.9	56.7	57.1	50.4	51.5	52.8	67.6
Other	57.7	61.6	57.1	60.5	55.5	57.4	57.1	54.8
Totals	57.4	62.5	57.7	59.1	55.4	55.5	56.5	58.8

Source: Data from Ragsdale 1996, table 8.10, calculated by author.
Note: See table 4.3 for legend.

Summary and Conclusion

The findings in this chapter reveal interesting similarities in average legislative support in the House for presidents' positions on legislative votes. Overall, presidents' vote positions obtain nearly 60 percent agreement in the House. Differences in support are clear between the two parties and across the individual presidents. Not surprisingly, Johnson was supported most and Reagan and Bush supported least. The latter were the only two presidents to drop below 50 percent overall support from House members, until Clinton in 1995.[13] The selected year in presidential term of office revealed very few differences in overall legislative support. Average percentage agreement with presidents is greatest during the first (honeymoon) year; support seems inevitably to decline when they are in a reelection or lame-duck (last) year in office.

The two substantive policy typologies also show differences in legislative support of the president. The two presidencies thesis is limited inherently by being a dichotomy rather than a broader-ranging typology, but some differences in support by domestic and foreign policy were evident. Foreign policy positions are less than four percentage points more likely to be supported by members of the House than are domestic positions. The two presidencies designation appeared to have little sensitivity overall but was useful when looking at presidents' party. Overall differences occurred only for Republicans, however, since House members' support for Democratic presidents barely differed by domestic or foreign policy. Among individual presidents, Ford and Reagan revealed the most and Johnson and Nixon the least variation in support between domestic and foreign policy, but no trend over time appears. Only the last year in presidents' term exhibited much variation in presidents' average support in the House between domestic and foreign policy.

Greater ranges in House support for presidents' positions were revealed in the King and Ragsdale designation. Presidents receive greatest average support for positions on trade policy and, as expected, party differences are particularly stark in social welfare and least in agriculture and foreign aid. Kennedy fared best among all presidents in trade, defense, and social welfare issues. Ford did much better in defense than in social welfare. Among the selected year aggregations, trade, defense, government, and social welfare did best during the first year in office while agriculture and foreign aid did worse then.

All in all, differences in overall legislative support of presidents' vote positions on all House roll call votes reveal interesting patterns. The two substantive typologies differentiated well, particularly King and Ragsdale, which revealed variation among the seven issue areas that were masked with the two presidencies dichotomy. Likewise, useful differentiation was offered by the political time groupings of the data (by presidential party, individual president, and year-in-presidential-term). Party was somewhat less discriminating for the support variable than it had been for position taking (see chap. 4). Among the time aggregations, individual presidents had better ability to differentiate support for presidents' vote positions than did either the presidents' political party or the selected year in their terms of office.

The CQ organization provides numerous measures of presidential relations with Congress. Key votes, success (both new and old), support, and the information accompanying these votes yield important data for scholars. But in failing to recognize the quite different nature of the indicators, authors have frequently used them interchangeably. Success originally was based on initiatives to Congress that come from presidents themselves. Support is also derived from legislative roll calls on which the president takes a position; thus, they are sponsored by Congress. Therefore, the support measure reflects member responses not to presidential policy but merely to his position on a particular issue before Congress. This chapter has found utility in all of the concepts, but scholars must keep in mind the conceptual and measurement differences, and also strengths and weaknesses, among these indicators in studying presidential-congressional relations.

CHAPTER 7

Presidential Executive Action

with Brad T. Gomez

Introduction

In this chapter, executive order issuance is examined as one form of decision making activity by presidents. Examples of dramatic orders include Franklin Roosevelt's internment of Japanese Americans in 1942, Harry Truman's desegregating the military in 1948, Richard Nixon's classifying sensitive national security information, and Ronald Reagan's limiting administrative regulation. Executive orders are "instruments of government authority" (Cooper 1986, 236) and are important actions despite receiving very little attention in the empirical literature (Utter and Cooper 1995). Although executive orders can serve purely routine (or administrative) functions, they may also have policy purposes. Executive orders issued as mechanisms of policy adoption are seemingly separate from the legislative process; yet, these presidential actions are likely influenced by interactions with Congress.

Nature of Executive Orders

Presidents make decisions in a highly charged political atmosphere. This is evident by the fact that most research on presidential decision making focuses on crisis situations, usually through the analysis of discrete actions (see, for example, Allison 1971).[1] However, crisis decisions often encompass many unique situations. Generalizable and perhaps predictable patterns of behavior may be more observable in the routine decisions that presidents must also make. Yet, scholars have seemingly found routine actions uninteresting, particularly less so than those made during international military crises. George Edwards and Stephen Wayne (1983) have decried the limited research on more routine decision making; as a result, few propositions and almost no general theories guide empirical research on presidential actions like executive orders.

Decision making is often conceptually difficult to define because researchers need to tap the varied personal and institutional constraints presidents face. Although many decisions might seem solitary, presidents rarely act as unitary actors. An early view of the presidency was Clinton Rossiter's (1956) depiction of the president "wearing many hats." However, even if one accepts such roles (for example, the president as "chief executive"), presidents seldom act without input and constraint from others. Indeed, a continuing controversy in the literature is whether to view presidents individually (Neustadt 1960; Barber 1992; Lowi 1985) or from an institutional perspective (King and Ragsdale 1988; Edwards, Kessel, Rockman 1993). Greg Hager and Terry Sullivan (1994) provide the best empirical test of this controversy to date, finding that institutional (presidency-centered) factors better explain presidents' public activities, but that individual (president-centered) variables also contribute to our knowledge. Thus, a mixed approach seems appropriate in examining executive order issuance.

Although institutional factors are important in decision making, presidents bring personal characteristics and preferences to the task as well. They may have strong orientations toward activism in policy-making and philosophical views about the proper role of government. Presidents also possess a variety of resources in performing the decision-making task. Richard Neustadt (1960) discusses numerous resources presidents have in policy-making, including persuasion, professional reputation, and public prestige. Subsequent authors have tried to theorize further about these components of power (Tatalovich and Daynes 1979; Cronin 1980, 130; Thomas 1977, 170). Others have sought to examine such factors empirically (Gleiber and Shull 1992; Kerbel 1991; Edwards 1989; Bond and Fleisher 1990).

Brad Gomez and Steven Shull (1995) find both personal and institutional aspects helpful in examining presidential decision making. They also doubt that such decisions are made from a single environmental perspective. Constraints on presidential action appear in the form of other authoritative decision makers who share policy-making functions with presidents. Political and institutional constraints come from all branches of government and throughout the political system. The legislative environment, including the incidence of divided government, influences presidential decision making. A recent example is Clinton's executive action to put together the Mexican economic bailout after congressional support collapsed.

Importance of Executive Orders

Executive orders are presidential decisions that technically have the same legal effect as legislative statute "if issued under a valid claim of authority and published" (Cooper 1986, 240).[2] They remain the law of the land unless overturned by act of Congress or subsequent executive order. However, a strict interpretation of the Constitution might preclude executive orders because they are a type of presidential legislation and, thus, an infringement on separation of powers. Yet, presidents have often cited the authority for executive orders as coming from the Constitution or legislation itself. The Supreme Court has allowed considerable legislative delegation to the president, therein upholding this device of presidential leadership, especially in foreign policy (Cooper 1986, 252).

Executive orders have long been used for narrow, routine administrative matters. Certainly that was the rule prior to World War II (Ragsdale 1993, 74). Since then, however, presidents increasingly have issued orders as broader instruments of policy as well. Philip Cooper asserts that their usage increased dramatically with presidential war and emergency power (1986, 236). Although executive orders have become an important instrument of presidential prerogative power, it is assumed that most still are issued for routine, administrative purposes (such as Clinton's order in 1996 adjusting pay rates) rather than to bring about large-scale policy change.

An interesting question arises over the purpose of executive orders, and presidents' motivations probably vary considerably. Orders may be issued in response to nonsupport for presidents' policy preferences in Congress, as an alternative form of policy *adoption* (Nathan 1983; Peterson 1990, 87). Such orders are designed to take new policy directions and may be fairly dramatic, resulting from a highly energized, controversial legislative environment. Others seem designed more to *implement* laws passed by Congress that presidents favor.[3] Examples include several Clinton orders early in 1993 to move quickly on legislation passed by a Democratic Congress that had been stymied by Republican presidents for twelve years. Thus, even when highly supported in Congress, presidents may issue orders to carry out specific rules for agencies to follow, which are necessary since lawmaking itself tends to be highly general (Kerwin 1994). These latter orders would be less policy oriented, less controversial, and more routine in scope, resulting largely from the executive environment. Dennis Gleiber and Shull (1992, 447–48) have discussed this dual nature of executive orders.

A third potential motivation may also exist. In a desire to change the role or growth of government, presidents may issue orders concerning reorganization or other routine *administrative* matters. These executive orders could have varied functions or purposes and might be less substantive and controversial than those falling within the seven policy areas. Obviously, these three motivations (adoption, implementation, administration) must be viewed as ideal types, given that goals behind executive order issuance are probably mixed. For example, orders that implement policy may also have administrative reorganization functions. Thus, executive orders likely have varied motivations, but these three designations may have conceptual utility.

This preliminary effort does not categorize executive orders according to these perceived motivations. Such an effort would probably require a detailed content analysis of the nearly 63 numbered executive orders issued annually. However, the preliminary findings in this chapter based upon related notions may reveal whether such a future enterprise, however time consuming, would be worthwhile.[4] For present purposes, presidential goals for order issuance are probably more implementation or administration than adoption when Congress supports their policy preferences (as in the previous Clinton example). As Neustadt (1960) suggests, the United States does not have separation of powers but more a "sharing of powers" between the executive and legislative branches. Thus, the legislative environment is important, and nonsupport by Congress probably requires the president with strong ideological preferences to respond in kind by adopting alternative policy. Thus, in instances of partisan or ideological conflict with Congress, a stronger policy motivation for presidents' decisions may exist.

The limited empirical research investigating executive order issuance is almost all in the realm of civil rights (Morgan 1970; Shull 1993, 107–11). This literature reveals that presidents have used executive orders within this policy realm for different reasons. Presidents Carter and Reagan were among the heaviest users of civil rights executive orders, although their policy preferences differed greatly (Shull 1993). One scholar finds that Carter used orders to seek greater representativeness and participation while Reagan used them as a device to reduce bureaucratic rule making (Kerwin 1994, 70). Research of this sort describes motivations and activities overall and occasionally by issue area but provides limited theoretical explanation for such decisions by presidents.

We suggest that executive order issuance is a function of presidents' legislative relations. Although orders may adopt alternative policy, presidents may also issue executive orders when they are not highly supported in Congress, as part of an "administrative presidency" strategy (Nathan 1983; Waterman 1989; Durant 1992). Yet evidence is mixed; a recent effort (Gomez and Shull 1995) finds the relationship between these two variables actually to be positive.[5] No other research has been conducted on the interrelationship of these legislative and executive actions or examining these orders according to groupings of political time and policy areas.

All in all, presidents have executive options in policy-making, but such motives and decisions also depend on the legislative environment they face. Presumably, presidents who are highly supported in Congress should have less need to issue executive orders, at least to adopt policy. Such an interpretation would argue that executive orders depend little upon the legislative environment. Rather, they are discretionary administrative actions that are largely a function of the executive environment. However, our preliminary study reveals that orders are issued within a legislative context. In addition, personal factors, like preferences and resources, may also influence such decision making. This analysis should help scholars assess these important linkages.

Conceptual and Measurement Concerns

Measuring Executive Orders

This research uses the average number of executive orders per year and, particularly, percentage by issue area, as another indicator of presidential-congressional relations. One may find executive orders in the *Federal Register* (as a requirement of Executive Order [EO] No. 10006 issued by Truman in 1948). Executive orders also appear in the *Codification of Presidential Proclamations and Executive Orders* and in the *Weekly Compilation of Presidential Documents* and, beginning with the Carter administration, the latter contains the same information as *Public Papers of the Presidents.* Shull (1993) and others used these sources to collect civil rights executive orders, but King and Ragsdale (1988) categorized all numbered orders into the seven substantive policy areas (which we then also group into the two presidencies dichotomy). These orders provide the data for this chapter.

King and Ragsdale also include non-policy-specific orders, including ceremonial/cultural, federalism, and personnel/agency requests. An example of a symbolic order is Clinton's establishing the Armed Forces Service Medal EO No. 12985, January 11, 1996. For present purposes, such orders are relegated to an "other" (nonpolicy—routine or administrative) category and included but deemphasized in this analysis. Executive orders are not categorized into the Lowi typology, but annual executive order issuance is compared to presidents' legislative support, assessing the use of orders as an alternative form of policy adoption.

Expectations for Executive Orders

Apart from being related to presidents' legislative support, other expectations are offered for executive order issuance. Although many orders are anticipated for Truman, who appears early in the study, executive order use generally should be less frequent in the contemporary period. Also, executive order issuance probably has changed by policy area over time as government has grown more complex in areas of trade, government, and resources. Among other policy areas, executive order issuance should be greater in areas traditionally deferred to more by Congress (e.g., foreign policy). Apart from increases in certain areas of foreign policy, presumably orders have increased over time in more routine domestic areas (e.g., government).

Contrary to earlier expectations on civil rights (Morgan 1970, 78–80;

Flaxbeard 1983, 12), Shull finds that Republicans, not Democrats, are more likely to issue civil rights orders (1989, 94). This tendency may not occur for other issue areas, however, and Gomez and Shull (1995) show that Democrats are more assertive. Republican presidents presumably emphasize foreign trade, defense, and government while Democratic presidents focus on foreign aid, resources, and social welfare. Because Democratic presidents are generally more assertive, they probably use this device to assert policy more than do Republicans. Very closely related to presidential party is the notion of divided government, where more order issuance should occur under divided rather than under unified government. Here again, such orders under divided government are probably more likely policy adoption rather than implementation or administration. Executive orders are the only activity included in which data exist for part of the Truman and all of the Eisenhower administrations.

Individual presidents will likely vary considerably in their utilization of executive orders. Because of the earlier finding by Gomez and Shull (1995), it is easy to hypothesize that presidents receiving greater legislative support (e.g., primarily Democrats) will also issue more executive orders. However, it is possible that support is not the operative variable but, rather, that individual president is the driving force. In other words, presidents who are assertive in taking vote positions could also be assertive in issuing executive orders. In any event, the expectation is that Truman, Carter, and Reagan will push many orders, the latter two due to the extensive regulatory efforts by both administrations in civil rights (Shull 1993). Conversely, Eisenhower, Ford, and Bush should issue few orders. Of course, the latter two presidents inherited the office from the vice presidency and had little inclination to adopt alternative policy. Individual president differences may also vary by policy areas.

Finally, executive order issuance should vary according to the selected year in presidents' terms of office. Because it was earlier asserted that presidents would be more assertive during their first and last year, more orders should occur during those years rather than during the reelection year. However, presidents presumably concentrate on legislation early but then turn to administrative solutions later in their term. Accordingly, executive orders should be issued with least frequency during their first year in office. Also, because domestic policy is given greater attention earlier in presidential administrations, orders in the foreign policy area should increase over their years in office.

Results of Analysis

The discussion begins with the average frequency overall of executive order issuance and by presidential party, then by individual president, and then by year in presidential term of office. For overall executive orders only, type of government (unified versus divided) can also be examined. The results for divided government differ only slightly from partisanship because only Truman differs from the pattern of divided government occurring only under Republican presidents during the years being analyzed (1947–94). This rich data set of executive orders exists for a much longer period, but many early ones are not numbered, as all are in more recent years, and, of course, are not coded by policy area by King and Ragsdale (1988).

Overall

The data for average executive order issuance are presented in table 7.1.Overall, presidents from Truman to Clinton average nearly 63 executive orders per year in office. Democratic presidents, often characterized as more active generally than Republicans, do indeed average many more orders annually (by 21.8 percentage points). This finding corresponds with the findings in chapter 6 that Democratic presidents were much more successful on their position taking on legislative votes than were Republicans. Therefore, Democrats probably are not issuing orders for independent executive policy adoption but rather to implement policies with which they agree. Also, Democratic

TABLE 7.1.   Mean Issuance of Executive Orders Per Year

Overall	62.6
By Party	
Republican	53.5
Democrat	75.3
Type of Government	
Divided	51.6
Unified	77.5
By President	
Truman	99.5
Eisenhower	59.8
Kennedy	76.0
Johnson	61.8
Nixon	59.2
Ford	50.7
Carter	77.7
Reagan	50.3
Bush	41.3
Clinton	55.0
By Year	
First	63.9
Last	60.8
Reelection	51.5
Other	63.6

Source: All executive order data for this chapter are complied from Ragsdale (1996, table 7.15).

presidents (except Truman) always had their partisan supporters in charge of both chambers of Congress. This fact relates to the dichotomous divided government variable, which does slightly better (at 25.9 percentage points) than party at differentiating executive order issuance.[6]

Great variation in average issuance of executive orders appears among the 10 modern presidents, as observed in table 7.1. Truman issued by far the most orders annually for the years in which data are available. With considerable falloff, Carter and Kennedy averaged the next most orders. It will surprise few observers that Bush and Ford issued few orders on average, but the fact that Reagan also was unlikely to issue orders does not square with observations of his assertiveness in the administrative presidency (Nathan 1983). Clinton was least likely to issue orders among modern Democratic presidents.[7] Generally, there appears a downward trend in executive order issuance over the period of this study.

Finally, few differences in average frequency of order issuance across selected year in presidents' term of office are also observable in table 7.1. The last year does not stand out in order issuance, and thus orders are seldom used to adopt alternative policies to legislation as presidents leave office. This finding is contrary to preliminary expectations. Presidents average the fewest orders during the reelection year. A possible explanation is the greater public attentiveness then and the fact that presidents might not wish to chance such visible actions.

As with position taking, the executive order data have been standardized by mean percentages by policy area for two reasons. The first is to control for the differing number of years available (by party, type of government, president, and year in term) that would be masked were simple frequency counts used. Second, percentages rather than raw numbers across policy areas make more sense theoretically. Thus, the analysis that follows, first by the two presidencies grouping and then by the King and Ragsdale typology, presents percentages of executive orders issued in each policy area of the total numbers of orders issued.

Two Presidencies

Overall, it can be seen in table 7.2 that presidents average significantly more executive orders (by 11.1 percentage points) in the domestic sphere than in foreign policy.[8] Obviously, part of this explanation is due to the passage of more domestic than foreign legislation, and, thus, many orders must implement or carry out such legislation. The same table shows, as expected, that the policy area issuance gap is greater for Democrats (who issue 16.8 percentage points' more domestic than foreign orders) than it is for Republicans (5.7 percentage points). Republican differences in order issuance by the two presidencies typology average about one-third that of Democrats.

The considerable differences in executive order issuance by presidents are further amplified when comparing domestic and foreign policy. Somewhat surprisingly, the differences are greatest for Nixon, who issued the greatest percentage of his orders among all presidents in the domestic realm (see table 7.3). Although this finding could result from his administrative presidency strategy (Nathan 1983), other literature shows that Nixon did not try to dismantle the Great Society; in fact, he expanded it in some areas (Ripley 1972). Thus, despite Nixon's foreign policy interests, he gave considerable attention to domestic matters. The other large differences are for Democratic presidents (Truman and, particularly, Kennedy and Clinton), who averaged many more domestic than foreign orders. Only two presidents issued more foreign than domestic orders (Reagan by a small margin and Bush by a large margin). Bush was clearly an outlier, showing a much clearer disdain for the domestic realm than *any* modern president.

Differences in executive order issuance by selected year are observable but perhaps are not as dramatic as for the other aggregations of the data. The most dramatic difference observable in table 7.4 is that only in the reelection year are more foreign than domestic orders issued. This finding squares with a common perception that presidents seeking reelection emphasize foreign policy to enhance their status as global leaders. Apart from the theoretically uninteresting "other" year, the greatest differences in order issuance are during the last year, where domestic orders averaged 12.5 percentage points more than foreign order issuance.

The findings in tables 7.2 through 7.4 reveal the utility of the two presidencies thesis. Most results were as expected: Democrats give relatively

TABLE 7.2. Mean Percentage of Executive Orders (two presidencies; by presidential party)

		Overall	Foreign	Domestic
Republican	%	99.7[a]	47.0	52.7
	N	(36.4)[b]	(17.1)	(19.2)
Democrat	%	100.0	41.6	58.4
	N	(55.0)[b]	(22.9)	(32.2)
Totals	%	100.0	44.4	55.5
	N	(44.1)[b]	(19.6)	(24.5)

Source: The data for Tables 7.2 and 7.3 combine the Ragsdale data from her seven categories in table 7.15.

[a]Overall percents may not equal 100 due to rounding.

[b]Ns are fewer for the two presidencies than with the overall figures in table 7.1 and the Ragsdale typology since the other (nonsubstantive) category is omitted here. The Ns in this and all remaining tables in the chapter are not whole numbers due to averaging them as number per year and then into policy and time groupings.

TABLE 7.3.   Mean Percentage of Executive Orders (two presidencies; by president)

President	Overall %[a]	Overall N[b]	Foreign %	Foreign N	Domestic %	Domestic N
HST	100.5	71.7	41.9	29.8	58.6	42.1
DDE	100.7	42.9	49.4	21.2	51.3	22.0
JFK	104.0	57.4	41.1	23.6	62.9	36.1
LBJ	99.9	41.6	42.8	17.8	57.2	23.8
RMN	99.8	35.7	31.4	11.2	68.4	24.4
GRF	101.4	29.0	49.3	14.3	52.1	15.1
JEC	100.3	53.5	44.7	23.9	55.6	29.8
RWR	100.2	38.6	51.0	19.7	49.2	19.0
GHWB	98.0	25.4	63.4	16.1	34.6	8.8
WJC	100.0	52.5	37.1	19.5	62.9	33.0
Totals	99.9	44.1	44.4	19.6	55.5	24.5

[a]Overall percentages may not equal 100 due to rounding.

[b]Ns are fewer for the two presidencies than with the overall figures in table 7.1 and the Ragsdale typology since the other (nonsubstantive) category is omitted here.

greater attention to domestic policy; Bush especially emphasized foreign policy; and presidents are more attentive to foreign policy executive orders during their reelection years. Although seemingly discretionary, presidents may choose not to emphasize highly visible domestic matters through execu-

TABLE 7.4.   Mean Percentage of Executive Orders (two presidencies; by year in term)

Year		Overall	Foreign	Domestic
First	%	100.0	45.4	54.6
	N	(44.7)[b]	(20.3)	(24.4)
Last	%	100.5[a]	44.0	56.5
	N	(42.2)[b]	(18.6)	(23.9)
Reelection	%	100.2[a]	52.3	47.9
	N	(33.1)[b]	(17.3)	(15.9)
Other	%	100.0	43.0	57.0
	N	(45.6)[b]	(19.6)	(26.0)
Totals	%	100.0	44.4	55.6
	N	(44.1)[b]	(19.6)	(24.5)

Source: Data from Ragsdale 1996, table 7.15, calculated by the author.

[a]Overall percentages may not equal 100 due to rounding.

[b]Ns are fewer for the two presidencies than with the overall figures in table 7.1 and the Ragsdale typology since the other (nonsubstantive) category is omitted here.

tive action when running for reelection. All in all, the two presidencies dichotomy was quite useful in understanding this important (but somewhat declining) administrative resource available to presidents.

King and Ragsdale Typology

Using the King and Ragsdale typology offers the advantage of disaggregating from the two presidencies dichotomy, thereby capturing potentially masked differences. However, a disadvantage arises in that the seven issue areas are very dissimilar in their frequency of executive order issuance. For example, foreign aid and agriculture each account for just over 1 percent of all executive orders, making few cases available for their analysis.[9] In addition, King and Ragsdale were unable to categorize nearly 30 percent of executive orders into any of the seven issue area designations. These residual orders are examined separately as a nonpolicy "other" category. They include orders simply amending earlier ones, which Clinton did 10 times in 1995 alone.

Table 7.5 reveals that, overall, three policy-specific areas (foreign trade, defense, and government) account for the bulk of executive orders (45.8 percent of all orders and 65.3 percent among the seven policy categorized orders). As mentioned earlier, orders in foreign aid and agriculture were much less frequent on average, with resources and social welfare falling in between them and the largest three groups in utilization. Republicans were much less likely to issue "other" (nonpolicy) orders compared to Democrats. The table reveals no substantial differences in emphasis by presidential party in most

TABLE 7.5. Mean Percentage of Executive Orders (King and Ragsdale; by presidential party)

Party	Overall	TR	AI	DF	SW	GO	RE	AG	Other[a]
Republican									
%	99.8[b]	15.3	1.3	15.3	7.1	15.5	11.6	1.3	2.0
N	(53.5)[c]	(8.2)	(.7)	(8.2)	(3.8)	(8.3)	(6.2)	(.9)	(17.1)
Democrat									
%	100.3[b]	14.3	.9	15.1	11.3	15.4	15.0	1.1	27.2
N	(75.3)[c]	(10.8)	(.7)	(11.4)	(8.5)	(11.6)	(11.3)	(.8)	(20.5)
Totals									
%	100.8[b]	14.9	1.1	15.3	9.1	15.5	13.3	1.4	29.7
N	(62.6)[c]	(9.3)	(.7)	(9.6)	(5.7)	(9.7)	(8.3)	(.9)	(18.6)

Source: Ragsdale 1996, table 7.15.

Note: See table 4.3 for legend.

[a]Equals ceremonial/cultural, federalism, personal/agency requests.

[b]Overall percentages do not equal 100 due to rounding.

[c]The *N*s in tables 7.5 through 7.7 are not whole numbers due to averaging them first as number per year and then into policy and time groupings.

issue areas (e.g., defense, government), but considerable party differences are evident in the social welfare issue area.[10]

Differences in executive order issuance across the seven issue areas also vary by individual president. Beginning first with nonsubstantive (and presumably more routine) orders, Ford emphasized them relatively the most and Clinton, by far, focused on them least (see table 7.6).[11] Reagan issued the greatest percentage of his orders on *trade* policy (27.0 percent) compared to Nixon who emphasized that issue least among modern presidents (9.3 percent). Due to very low numbers, differences in foreign *aid* issuance are few, with Bush issuing relatively the most by far (4.4 percent of his orders) compared with none for Truman, Nixon, and Clinton. *Defense* reveals considerable variation in order issuance (25.3 percent for Eisenhower to just 6.8 percent for Carter). *Social welfare* also shows major differences, with percent-

TABLE 7.6. Mean Percentage of Executive Orders (King and Ragsdale; by president)

President	Overall[a]	TR	AI	DF	SW	GO	RE	AG	Other[a]
Truman	100.2	10.4	0	19.6	5.8	18.1	18.1	.3	27.9
	(99.5)	(10.3)	(0)	(19.5)	(5.8)	(18.0)	(18.0)	(.3)	(27.8)
Eisenhower	100.5	8.9	1.3	25.3	4.3	15.9	13.5	3.0	28.3
	(59.8)	(5.3)	(.8)	(15.1)	(2.6)	(9.5)	(8.1)	(1.8)	(16.9)
Kennedy	102.9	7.9	1.7	21.4	11.4	19.3	14.5	2.2	24.5
	(76.0)	(6.0)	(1.3)	(16.3)	(8.7)	(14.7)	(11.0)	(1.7)	(18.6)
Johnson	100.0	14.2	1.3	13.3	12.9	12.0	11.7	1.9	32.7
	(61.8)	(8.8)	(.8)	(8.2)	(8.0)	(7.4)	(7.2)	(1.2)	(20.2)
Nixon	99.9	9.0	0	9.6	9.8	15.7	14.4	1.4	39.7
	(59.2)	(5.5)	(0)	(5.7)	(5.8)	(9.3)	(8.5)	(.8)	(23.5)
Ford	100.9	17.2	.6	10.5	7.3	9.3	13.2	0	42.8
	(50.7)	(8.7)	(.3)	(5.3)	(3.7)	(4.7)	(6.7)	(0)	(21.7)
Carter	100.5	22.3	1.7	6.8	16.1	8.4	13.5	.4	31.3
	(77.7)	(17.3)	(1.3)	(5.3)	(12.5)	(6.5)	(10.5)	(.3)	(24.3)
Reagan	99.2	27.0	1.6	10.5	8.9	19.9	7.2	.8	23.3
	(50.3)	(13.6)	(.8)	(5.3)	(4.5)	(10.5)	(3.6)	(.4)	(11.7)
Bush	98.9	18.9	4.4	15.7	4.4	6.1	8.5	2.4	38.5
	(41.3)	(7.8)	(1.8)	(6.5)	(1.8)	(2.5)	(3.5)	(1.0)	(15.9)
Clinton	100.3	20.0	0	15.5	14.0	27.3	19.1	.9	4.5
	(55.0)	(11.0)	(0)	(8.5)	(7.7)	(15.0)	(10.5)	(.5)	(2.5)
Totals									
%	100.8	14.8	1.1	15.3	9.1	15.5	13.3	1.4	29.7
N	(62.1)	(9.3)	(.7)	(9.6)	(5.7)	(9.7)	(8.3)	(.9)	(18.6)

Source: Ragsdale 1996, table 7.15.

Note: See table 4.3 for legend. Figures in parentheses are base *N*s for the expressed percentages.

[a]Overall percentages may not equal 100 due to rounding.

ages of over 16 percent for Carter to just 4.4 percent for Bush (see table 7.6). Orders in the *government* dimension were used extensively by Kennedy (19.3 percent) but were only 6.1 percent of Bush's total orders. *Resources* orders (such as recreational fisheries in 1995) were emphasized heavily by Clinton (17.5 percent) and Truman (18.1) but hardly at all by Reagan (7.2 percent). *Agriculture* orders are rare; Eisenhower devoted 3.0 percent of his orders to them but Ford issued not a single one. These findings indicate that presidents' personal policy preferences matter.

Finally, selected year designations also distinguish executive order issuance across the King and Ragsdale typology (see table 7.7). A much higher percentage of trade orders are issued in the reelection than in the last year in office. Differences in foreign aid are fewer, but higher percentages are issued during the first than the last year. Differences in defense orders are not as great as those for trade, but greater percentages appear in the last than during the reelection year. Surprisingly, social welfare order issuance varies little across designated years, and the differences are not statistically significant. Government orders are much more likely during the last than the reelection year, lending credence to the suspicion that their utilization serves the purpose of reorganizing government as presidents leave office. Presidents would not wish to engender such controversy during a reelection campaign. No important differences occur in resource order issuance by selected year, but differences do emerge in agriculture, where a higher percentage of orders occur in the first year than during the other two selected year designations.

TABLE 7.7. Mean Percentage of Executive Orders (King and Ragsdale; by year in term)

Year	Overall	TR	AI	DF	SW	GO	RE	AG	Other[a]
First	100.1[b]	16.0	1.3	14.6	9.4	14.1	13.1	1.6	30.0
	(63.9)	(10.2)	(.8)	(9.3)	(6.0)	(9.0)	(8.4)	(1.0)	(19.2)
Last	100.4[b]	12.8	.4	17.3	7.1	17.3	14.5	.4	30.6
	(60.8)	(7.8)	(.3)	(10.5)	(4.3)	(10.5)	(8.8)	(.3)	(18.6)
Reelection	100.0	20.0	1.0	12.6	8.3	10.1	12.0	.3	35.7
	(51.5)	(10.3)	(.5)	(6.5)	(4.3)	(5.2)	(6.2)	(.2)	(18.4)
Other	100.2[b]	13.8	1.3	15.7	9.3	16.7	13.2	1.6	28.6
	(63.6)	(8.8)	(.8)	(10.0)	(5.9)	(10.6)	(8.4)	(1.0)	(18.2)
Totals	100.8[b]	14.9	1.1	15.3	9.1	15.5	13.3	1.4	29.7
	(62.6)	(9.3)	(.7)	(9.6)	(5.7)	(9.7)	(8.3)	(.9)	(18.6)

Note: See table 4.3 figure legend. Figures in parentheses are base *N*s for the expressed percentages.
[a]Equals ceremonial/cultural, federalism, personal/agency requests.
[b]Overall percentages may not equal 100 due to rounding.

Summary and Conclusion

This conclusion begins with some general findings about executive order issuance, revealing the utility of grouping these data by policy areas and political time. Overall, presidents issue on average nearly 63 executive orders annually. Democrats issue more orders than Republicans, and an even higher percentage occurs under unified than divided government. Among individual presidents, Truman and Carter issued many, as expected, but Reagan was not as assertive as the administrative presidency thesis would suggest (Nathan 1983). As found for assertiveness in position taking, presidents also issue relatively more executive orders during the first than during the reelection year in particular.

Policy area differences were quite pronounced, but some of the expectations were supported while others were not. Beginning with the two presidencies dichotomy, as anticipated, orders are more likely in domestic than in foreign policy. Democrats do issue a higher percentage of domestic executive orders than do Republicans. Reagan and Bush, particularly, issued greater percentages of executive orders in the foreign than the domestic realm. Certainly the latter is not surprising, given Bush's near disdain for budget and economic policy (Rockman 1991, 22). Foreign policy orders are more likely during the reelection year, and proportionately more domestic orders occur during the last year in office. Presidents probably need to issue more orders in the domestic realm as alternative means of policy adoption, while their greater legislative support in foreign policy suggests they use such orders to carry out legislation with which they agree, or for routine administration.

The King and Ragsdale seven-part typology also uncovered many differences in order issuance. Unfortunately, the frequencies are very small for two of the issue areas (foreign aid and agriculture) so any conclusions about them are problematic. At the other extreme were trade, defense, and government, where the highest percentages of orders were issued. As expected, a big party difference occurred for social welfare, but partisanship was muted on most other issue areas, especially government. Ford issued proportionately the most nonsubstantive orders (other category) while Clinton was much more policy oriented (lowest percentage in other category). Other individual president variations in emphases were also considerable: Eisenhower on defense, Kennedy on government, Reagan on trade, Clinton on resources. Finally, the selected year in presidents' term revealed different emphases: first year = social welfare, agriculture; last year = defense and government; reelection year = trade.

Almost no systematic research exists on executive order issuance per se, but because the legislative environment appears to be an important influence in the president's propensity to use this device that arena is emphasized heavily. This is particularly the case with legislative support, for which con-siderable research exists and which we found to be related to executive order issuance. Indeed, Gomez and Shull (1995) observe in related research that legislative support was among the most important influences on the frequency of executive orders. On average, presidents receiving the most support also issue the most executive orders.

Related to this finding, Democratic presidents appear to be using executive orders as a tool for implementing laws adopted by Congress with which they agree. This is because when they are supported they issue more orders and, thus, have less need than Republicans to adopt alternative policies auton-omously. When not supported in Congress, presidents are most likely moti-vated to use executive orders as alternative policy adoption. When receiving high levels of support, presidents apparently issue orders to provide more specific rules and administrative routine to carry out the legislation. Because of these seemingly varied motivations and roles for executive orders, policy areas and political time help to reveal these strategies available to presidents.

CHAPTER 8

Conclusion

Overview

Presidential-Congressional Relations has examined relations between the president and Congress in several aspects of adopting public policy. Virtually all existing research examines such relations using only legislative support and/or success or modifications of these two variables. Four types of activities are covered in this book: presidential position taking, controversy over congressional votes, legislative support of the president, and executive order issuance. The three components other than support have received little systematic attention from scholars of presidential-congressional relations. Such interactions within these four venues are examined using political time and policy area approaches.

Presumably, presidents exert greatest influence in position taking and executive order issuance, while Congress plays the most important role in legislative controversy and in deciding whether to approve presidents' roll call vote positions. However, such a perspective is too simple. The environment in Congress constrains presidential preferences and actions, even presidents' adoption of policy in the form of executive orders. Despite roles for each actor, neither is without influence in any aspect of policy adoption. Besides, numerous interactions occur that ultimately affect such policies. The first part of this chapter summarizes some of these findings.

Typologies of public policy were hypothesized to reveal important differences on the activities of the presidential-congressional relations just analyzed. The three typologies incorporated (Aaron Wildavsky's two presidencies thesis, the Gary King and Lyn Ragsdale categorization, and the Theodore Lowi typology) have all been used before, but no one has compared all three in any systematic fashion. They all offer utility in that variation appears with each of the three for particular activities. Indeed, it is difficult to decide which one has the best explanatory power, but this preliminary effort suggests that, for now, none should be discounted when studying presidential-congressional relations.

Presidential-Congressional Relations incorporates yet another aggregation of the data. Although data are reported for the period 1957–94 (beginning

with 1949 for executive orders), these individual years are not of much interest. Rather, groupings of years offer greater theoretical utility by suggesting
patterns of political time according to presidential party, individual president,
and the selected year in presidential term of office. Sometimes the two types
of aggregation (by political time and policy areas) limit the number of data
points for any particular analysis. Therefore, caution is urged in interpreting
some of the results, but political time is also a valuable approach.

The second major section of this chapter delves into the implications for
the research. A number of data collection difficulties are considered in interpreting what some of the interesting results may mean. The focus is on both
the problems and prospects uncovered and what they may suggest for presidential-congressional interactions. This final section is concerned largely with
the utility of what has been uncovered for studying actor relations. In short,
how useful are the type of legislation, the three policy typologies, and three
groupings of political time in understanding these four dimensions of presidential-congressional interactions?

Summary of Results by Government Activities

The relationship between the president and Congress is exceedingly important
but not always easy to discern. As with most research, what is uncovered
depends upon the theory and measurement employed. Only one of the four
activities used in this research has been analyzed extensively; other measures
merit attention as well. This book shows how particular indicators and operationalizations were developed and utilized. Some analyses herein examined
only important legislation while others focused on all legislation. For the
latter, roll call votes in the House only were used, while votes in both chambers were compiled for important legislation.

The study expresses confidence that votes on important legislation are a
useful subset, differing in many respects from all roll call votes. Votes on final
passage of important legislation varied significantly by chamber, policy areas,
and political time aggregations. Unlike David Mayhew's (1992) data, which
are almost exclusively domestic, a roughly equal proportion of foreign legislation was added by using data based upon Barbara Hinckley's (1994) work.
Mayhew observed relatively more important legislation passing during the
middle years of the study (Richard Nixon through Jimmy Carter) rather than
before or since. He also found little difference in such passage according to
whether government is divided or unified (or by presidential party). However,
this study's use of votes on final passage of important legislation produced
some interesting results. Also, observable differences between important and
all votes emerged, as discussed next according to the four government activities.

Presidential Position Taking

Position taking is a response by presidents to legislative votes appearing in Congress. As has been shown, presidents cannot introduce legislation in Congress but certainly can express preferences on roll call votes on Congress's agenda. Position taking obviously is discretionary for presidents, however, so considerable variation occurs in this activity among individual presidents. First, presidents take positions twice as often on important as on all legislation. The reader will recall, however, that only final passage votes are included for the former, while many routine procedural or amendment votes may appear for the latter. Major policy area and political time differences occurred in presidential position taking.

Position taking occurs relatively more frequently in domestic than foreign policy and, as expected, partisan differences emerge as well. As expected, Democrats do emphasize the former relatively more and Republicans the latter relatively more. Such party differences are more pronounced for important legislation than for all legislation. Illustrating how the two presidencies thesis may miss variation, position taking averaged greatest in defense and resources and least in foreign aid and agriculture. Perhaps not surprising given research showing presidential emphasis in redistributive policy, position taking averaged greatest there and least on distributive policy, in which presidents presumably have least interest (Shull 1983; Spitzer 1983).

Obviously, considerable differences in position taking occur among the individual presidents. Probably no one would be surprised that John Kennedy and Lyndon Johnson took the greatest average frequency of positions on both important and all legislation. Dwight Eisenhower and Ronald Reagan averaged the least positions per year in office; but as a percentage of roll call votes, Gerald Ford took by far the fewest positions on average of any modern president. Somewhat unexpectedly, position taking on House votes occurs relatively least often during presidents' first year in office. Perhaps presidents are too busy then to concern themselves with many routine matters as they concentrate on their own agenda during the crucial honeymoon period. Early on, welfare reform was of interest to Bill Clinton, but after two vetoes a compromise plan was finally agreed to in August 1996 late during his reelection year.

Legislative Vote Controversy

In examining controversy on legislative votes, several (often very different) indicators were provided for important legislation, while a single partisan difference measure was included for all House votes. The results of the five controversy measures on important legislation diverged greatly, and interpretation sometimes was difficult. Considerable chamber differences occurred on important legislation votes (e.g., the Senate had more voice votes and more amendments but less vote splitting and a smaller percentage of partisan votes than did the House). Final passage votes on important legislation generate many amendments, but less than half of these votes were nonunanimous and less than one-quarter were partisan. However, partisan and nonunanimous voting actually occurred less often when Republicans rather than Democrats were presidents. Although voice voting was greater under Democratic presidents, no presidential party difference appeared in amendment frequency.

Individual president differences also were considerable on important legislation votes. Among contemporary presidents, the most vote controversy occurred under Bill Clinton in terms of percentage of partisan votes, non-unanimous votes, and average vote splitting. Despite Republican congressional agenda leadership, institutional controversy was high during the 104th Congress (1995–96). A president's first year was most partisan, containing the most nonunanimous votes and the highest percentage of vote splitting. Relatively more voice votes but fewer amendments occurred in foreign policy, as expected, but more vote splitting and about the same percentage of partisan votes appeared as in domestic policy. Agriculture had the lowest percentage of voice votes, the greatest percentage of partisan votes, and the greatest vote splitting, while resources was lowest on these indicators. Social welfare was not very controversial on any of the five conflict measures.

Tables 8.1 and 8.2 summarize these findings on position taking and controversy on important legislation in the form of rankings. These tables reflect relative attention or salience across government activities. On *position taking*, the lower number reflects greater assertiveness (e.g., 1 ranks higher than a 2). On *controversy*, a low number reflects the least disagreement (e.g., 1 ranks higher than 2).[1] Note that in table 8.1 using year groupings both position taking and controversy were greater under Democratic than Republican presidents. As expected, Johnson had the highest rank (lowest number) on these two indicators averaged, while Reagan ranked lowest (highest mean number). Obvious differences between the two activities were evident. Clinton, for example, was assertive in position taking but experienced greatest controversy. Major disagreements over funding during 1996 continued long after the fiscal year began. Differences by selected year were dramatic only for the last (lame-duck) year, which rank highest both on position taking and controversy.

The results in table 8.2 by policy areas can be compared to the political time groupings from table 8.1. Domestic policy is more salient in position taking (greater) and controversy (less) than foreign policy. Differences also appear by the King and Ragsdale typology, where four of the issues (defense, government, social welfare, and resources) rank highest in salience (greatest mean position taking and least controversy). Foreign aid, foreign trade, and, particularly, agriculture rank lowest on these two variables. When examining

TABLE 8.1. Rank Ordering of Government Activities on Important Legislation (by political time)

Aggregation	Position Taking	Controversy	$\overline{X}$	Overall
Party				
Republican	2	1	3/2	1.5
Democrat	1	2	3/2	1.5
President				
Eisenhower	8	4	12/2	6.0
Kennedy	2	5	7/2	3.5
Johnson	1	3	4/2	2.0
Nixon	6	1	7/2	3.5
Ford	5	8	13/2	6.5
Carter	4	7	11/2	5.5
Reagan	9	4	15/2	7.5
Bush	7	2	9/2	4.5
Clinton	3	9	12/2	6.0
Year				
First	2	4	6/2	3.0
Last	1	1	2/2	1.0
Reelection	4	3	7/2	3.5
Other	3	2	5/2	2.5

Note: Position taking refers to frequency per year in office. *Controversy* is based on the mean vote split indicator; the lower the number, the higher the rank (e.g., 1 = greatest position taking but least controversy).

TABLE 8.2. Rank Ordering of Government Activities on Important Legislation (by policy areas)

Policy Area	Position Taking	Controversy	$\overline{X}$	Overall
Two Presidencies				
Foreign	2	2	4/2	2.0
Domestic	1	1	2/2	1.0
King and Ragsdale				
Trade	6	5	11/2	5.5
Aid	5	7	12/2	6.0
Defense	2	4	6/2	3.0
Social Welfare	3	3	6/2	3.0
Government	4	2	6/2	3.0
Resources	1	3	4/2	2.0
Agriculture	7	6	13/2	6.5
Lowi				
Distributive	4	4	8/2	4.0
Regulatory	3	1	4/2	2.0
Redistributive	1	3	4/2	2.0
Constituent	2	2	4/2	2.0

Note: Position taking refers to frequency per year in office. *Controversy* is based on the mean vote split indicator; the lower the number, the higher the rank (e.g., 1 = greatest position taking but least controversy).

the Lowi typology, it is clear that only distributive policy is unique: it ranks highest on controversy but lowest on position taking. The other three categories are less discerning for important legislation votes. Subsequent tables make these same comparisons for all legislation in the House.

The measure of controversy for all legislation was a comparison of in- versus out-party House member support grouped by years and policy areas. This party gap in support was greater for Democratic than Republican legislators, suggesting that House members are more partisan when Republican presidents occupy the White House. However, Democrats, on average, have larger majorities and do not appear as hard on Republicans as GOP members are on Democratic presidents (Gibson 1995). The greatest average difference in party support occurred under Kennedy and the least under Nixon. Obviously, Republicans were strongly opposed to many Kennedy initiatives, but Democrats were nearly as supportive of Nixon's policies as were Republican House members. Selected year differences in party support averaged least during the last year in presidents' terms of office. In- versus out-party support differences were not great between domestic and foreign policy. Some mean differences occurred by the King and Ragsdale policy typology, but they too were not very dramatic.

Legislative Support of the President

Virtually all of the empirical literature on presidential-congressional relations focuses on presidents' legislative support or success. Considerable confusion exists in the literature over these indicators, and they measure quite different phenomena. Percentage agreement in the House with presidents' vote positions is utilized here. Overall, presidents are supported 60 percent in the House, but Democrats receive much greater support than Republicans. Johnson received the greatest and Reagan the least overall support from members of the House. Clinton's support was high in 1993–94 but then dropped to the lowest ever in 1995 before returning to a moderate level in 1996. The selected year in presidential term was not very useful in tapping president's legislative support in the House of Representatives.

As anticipated, foreign policy receives somewhat greater levels of support than domestic policy, but variation by policy area occurred only for Republican presidents. Not surprisingly, Johnson (highest) and Reagan (lowest) were the extremes in domestic policy support. Although Clinton's support was low in 1995, such domestic positions as job training and eliminating the Interstate Commerce Commission were upheld by Congress. Only in foreign policy do year groupings make much difference; in the last year presidents receive much greater foreign policy support than during other years. Within the King and Ragsdale typology, support was greatest for trade and least for aid and agriculture. Considerable party differences occurred in social welfare, as anticipated. Individual president variations were even greater than presidential party and the selected year within presidential term.

Executive Order Issuance

Some might assume that executive order issuance involves little presidential-congressional interaction. However, this analysis reveals that is not the case, and such orders provide another measure of presidential assertiveness *in a legislative environment.* Unlike what Shull observed in civil rights (1993, 111), Democratic presidents average more orders over all issues per year than do Republicans. Clearly related to party, more orders occur on average under unified than under divided government. Harry Truman issued by far the most orders annually, and Reagan averaged the fewest on average among modern presidents. Accordingly, the overall trend in order issuance is down somewhat through Clinton. Another finding was that presidents issue more orders during their first than during any other year in their terms.

When examining policy areas, Democratic presidents especially issue relatively more orders in domestic than foreign policy. Mean domestic order issuance was high for Kennedy and Clinton but low for Reagan and Bush, who focused more on foreign policy concerns. More surprising than this finding is the high percentage of domestic orders by Nixon. Foreign policy orders are issued relatively most often during presidents' reelection years, and domestic orders appear relatively most often during the last year in office.

Most executive orders classified by the King and Ragsdale typology on average occur in trade, defense, and government while the fewest occur relatively in foreign aid and agriculture. Social welfare order issuance varied greatly by presidential party, while government (presumably more routine matters) did not. The individual presidents had particular relative emphases (e.g., Eisenhower = defense; Reagan = trade, Clinton = resources). During the first year, welfare and agriculture were emphasized; during the last year, defense and government were prominent; during the reelection year, trade received considerable attention by presidents in executive order issuance.

Assessment

A large number of findings have been presented in this book and summarized in the previous sections. Similar to important legislation, tables 8.3 and 8.4 rank the four government activities available for all votes in the House of Representatives and executive order issuance by political time and policy areas. In table 8.3, the lower number (higher average ranking) overall for Democrats shows that these concerns were more salient for them than for

Republican presidents. That is, Democrats were more assertive in position taking and executive order issuance than Republican presidents. Democrats had greater legislative support but, unlike for important legislation, also experienced greater controversy on all House roll call votes. Perhaps surprisingly, Carter edges out Clinton and Johnson in overall mean assertiveness or salience, due primarily to the highly discretionary position taking and executive order issuance activities. Not surprisingly, Ford (with Reagan and Bush slightly trailing) was least assertive on average in the legislative arena. The first year was more salient for presidents than was their reelection year. They must make their mark early (hence the former) and seem too preoccupied to be very assertive in the latter.

Table 8.4 makes similar comparisons to table 8.3 on political time but by policy area emphases. Absolutely no difference occurs by the two presidencies notion, where two of the variables were more salient in foreign policy on average, while the other two show greater mean assertiveness in domestic

TABLE 8.3. Rank Ordering of Government Activities on All Legislation (by political time)

Aggregation	Position Taking	Controversy	Support	Executive Order Issuance	$\overline{X}$	Overall Rank
Party						
Republican	2	1	2	4	7/4	2.0
Democrat	1	2	1	1	5/4	1.3
President						
Eisenhower	8	2	6	4	20/4	5.0
Kennedy	7	9	2	2	21/4	5.3
Johnson	3	8	1	3	14/4	3.8
Nixon	6	1	4	5	16/4	4.0
Ford	9	4	7	7	27/4	7.8
Carter	1	5	5	1	12/4	3.0
Reagan	5	6	9	8	28/4	7.0
Bush	2	7	8	9	28/4	7.0
Clinton	4	3	3	6	16/4	4.0
Year						
First	4	3	1	1	9/4	2.3
Last	3	1	3	3	10/4	2.5
Reelection	2	2	4	4	12/4	3.0
Other	1	4	2	2	9/4	2.3

Note: Position taking refers to frequency per year in office. *Controversy* is based on the in- versus out-party support indicator. *Support* refers to the average percentage agreement in the House with the presidents' vote positions. *Executive orders* refer to the average number of executive orders issued per year. The lower the number, the higher the rank (e.g., 1 = greatest position taking, support, and executive order issuance but least controversy).

policy. However, dramatic differences may be seen by the King and Ragsdale issue areas. Trade and defense matters clearly receive greatest average attention by Congress and presidents. Agriculture is by far the least salient issue area of the seven used by King and Ragsdale. In fact, because this issue area contains so few cases, it is questionable whether it warrants being used as a separate category of public policy.

Implications of the Study

In this second major section of the chapter, the importance of the research is examined. The order of the discussion remains the same: considering the government activities first, then the groupings of these data by political time and policy areas. Before that exercise, however, the utility of studying important legislation in comparison to all legislation is discussed. As with all of these concepts, scholars should not be wedded to particular indicators, variables, data, or analysis techniques. Just because legislative success, for example, is available and widely used does not mean that it always should be. Other measures may be more relevant to the particular research question of interest. That should drive the research more than data availability and existing usage.

TABLE 8.4. Rank Ordering of Government Activities on All Legislation (by policy areas)

Policy Area	Position Taking	Controversy	Support	Executive Order Issuance	$\overline{X}$	Overall Rank
Two Presidencies						
Foreign	2	1	1	2	6/4	1.5
Domestic	1	2	2	1	6/4	1.5
King and Ragsdale						
Trade	6	1	1	3	9/4	2.3
Aid	5	3.5	4	7	18.5/4	4.6
Defense	4	3.5	2	2	11.5/4	2.9
Social Welfare	2	5	7	5	19/5	4.8
Government	1	7	6	1	15/4	3.8
Resources	3	2	5	4	14/4	3.5
Agriculture	7	6	3	6	22/4	5.5

Note: Position taking refers to frequency per year in office. *Controversy* is based on the in- versus out-party support indicator. *Support* refers to the average percentage agreement in the House with the presidents' vote positions. *Executive orders* refers to the average number of executive orders issued per year. The lower the number, the higher the rank (e.g., 1 = greatest position taking, support, and executive order issuance but least controversy).

Utility of Important Legislation

This research finds that important legislation is uniquely different from all legislation and that useful information about presidential-congressional relations may be gleaned from both sources of data. Important legislation is a much more manageable data set, particularly the analysis of the 617 roll call votes and 138 voice votes on final passage of legislation during the 1957–94 period. Obviously, such final passage votes are not completely comparable to the complete set of House votes provided by King and Ragsdale. Although an arduous task, scholars could collect only the final passage votes on all legislation (even if in only one chamber) for a closer comparison. The rationale here is that important legislation can be defined during the entire period and, despite greater frequency during the 1970s, its occurrence is relatively constant across time. Some anomalies occurred: for example, relatively more important legislation was adopted during presidents' last year in office than during any other year designation. The number of all votes, however, has greatly increased over time, and research shows that in some periods of this research they are dominated by amendments. Studies reveal that amendments do indeed differ from other roll call votes (Rohde 1994; Shull and Klemm 1987). Further comparisons of important and all votes are needed.

Utility of Government Activities

Presidential position taking on legislative votes provided the most direct comparison of important and all legislation. This variable is the denominator for both the current CQ support and success scores. The numerators of these two indicators are, of course, quite different and have been widely used in empirical research on presidential-congressional relations. Scholars have not examined position taking itself very much, and this book argues that it is an important indicator of presidential assertiveness in the legislative arena in its own right. It performed at least as well as any of the other activities in confirming expectations, which provides at least some face validity. Position taking varies greatly by important and all legislation and is a useful indicator of joint presidential-congressional policy-making.

Presidential assertiveness does not exist in a vacuum, however, and may be quite dependent on the legislative environment. Certainly one component of that environment is controversy over recorded votes. Because Chamber differences were dramatic enough on the numerous indicators of controversy, Senate and House comparisons are warranted, both for votes on important legislation and for those on all legislation. Such an enterprise as recording Senate votes by issue area, like King and Ragsdale do for the House, would be a first step toward examining chamber variations. Collecting roll calls just on final passage of legislation is feasible and, of course, the actual number of such roll call votes would be somewhat fewer in the upper chamber due to greater voice voting there on enacting legislation.

The more immediate task is to deal with the disparities in the five indicators of controversy on important legislation and to devise additional ones for all votes. The difficulty of creating an index of these scores, making certain to include both dimensions of vote margin and the partisan nature of such votes, has already been addressed. The mean vote split indicator appears to be the most useful for present purposes but, as mentioned earlier, scholars should choose indicators designed for their particular research questions. Vote margins and the partisan nature of all votes can be calculated since the roll calls are on-line,[2] and several related measures, such as Edwards's (1989) non-unanimous indicator, have already been used.

Support has received much attention heretofore, but confusion reigns between it and old and newer measures of success. None are inherently better than others, and each have useful purposes. First, CQ should state unequivocally that its newer measure of success (proportion of presidents' vote positions that prevail) is quite different from its earlier box score measure once designated as success (proportion of presidents' legislative requests or initiatives that are approved by Congress).[3] Additionally, Ragsdale (1996) should provide scholars with the numerators (raw numbers of times Congress as a whole or number of members approving of the presidents' vote positions).[4] Such values are needed for both indicators rather than simply reporting the resulting percentages by year. Obviously, those data should also be provided by the seven issue areas used. As it now stands, scholars are limited to averaging mean percentages when aggregating the data beyond the particular calendar year.

The final governmental activity examined in this work was executive order issuance, again aggregated by political time and policy areas. Like position taking, executive order issuance has received almost no systematic attention from scholars. What little empirical research that has occurred has been in the realm of civil rights policy (Shull 1993). Like position taking, issuing executive orders is a type of assertiveness by presidents that seemingly should be removed from the legislative arena. However, it is related to legislative support ($r = .453$), and it is also related to position taking ($r = .372$). Because presidents issuing executive orders are also highly supported by Congress, they appear to be using them as a way of implementing legislation with which they agree or for routine matters rather than seeking alternative policy adoption.

Obviously, the four government activities examined are not the only interactions between the president and Congress. Other important venues include informal relations like legislative liaison and more formal interactions like budgeting and the veto. Agenda setting is also important, where both change and continuity have been observed according to political time and policy areas. For example, during the Cold War period, neither actor could ignore the Soviet Union, and defense policy received great attention. Perhaps inevitably, presidents played a greater role than Congress in such policies. During the post–Cold War period, neither actor could ignore the growing deficit, which greatly constrained their actions. Still, the 104th Congress tried very hard to assert its own domestic agenda against a weakened Bill Clinton in 1995–96. Nevertheless, LeLoup and Shull (1993) show that throughout the post–World War II period, leadership by both actors was possible in all policy areas and often necessary to avoid deadlock in governing.

Utility of Political Time

In general, the aggregations of data by political time performed about as well as when the policy typologies were used. Indeed, although both are dichotomies, presidential party usually was more discriminating than was the two presidencies. Partisanship of course is increasing in congressional voting, and Democratic and Republican presidents and legislators do seem to behave quite differently. On most of the government activities, significant party differences emerged; sometimes they were amplified when used in conjunction with the policy typologies. Democratic presidents on average were more assertive, had more support, but also had more controversy on votes than Republican presidents. Admittedly, presidential party may be a poor surrogate for presidential ideology, but studies have found the two strongly related (Gleiber and Shull 1992; Gomez and Shull 1995). Yet ideology is a useful concept too, and CQ should resume (since 1991) providing the votes used for determining individual legislator scores for each of four different organizations. Without the votes themselves, it is much more difficult to tap presidential ideology.

Individual president variations were also quite stark. A problem of few observations may appear when grouping data by nine presidents (ten with executive orders). This was particularly true for Ford and Clinton, for which just two years of data were available. Presidents who were assertive with Congress (like Kennedy, Johnson, and Clinton) were also highly supported, largely due to favorable partisan majorities in both chambers. The former two (but not Clinton) also issued many executive orders, yet the three differed greatly in controversy between votes on important versus all legislation. The five Republican presidents during the 1957–94 period (Eisenhower, Nixon, Ford, Reagan, and Bush) generally were least assertive and supported least by Congress.

The year in term generally produced the least satisfying results.[5] Some observations are clear in that presidents usually get their way earlier rather than later in their terms of office. The first (honeymoon) year was lowest in controversy on important legislation but greatest in support on all legislation and executive order issuance. Last (lame-duck) and reelection years, while similar to each other as expected, were not always greatly different from the first year. Position taking and controversy were greater in the last year for important legislation as was controversy for all House votes. Reelection year did not emerge as greatly different on any indicators.

Using political time in this volume goes beyond standard treatments. It represents a new way of thinking about presidential-congressional relations according to recurring cycles instead of purely chronological time. The concern is more with understanding patterns and meaning in relationships between the two institutions. In addition to political party and individual presidents, the selected year within president's term of office facilitates comprehension of stability and change in agendas and activities. It allows for a more sophisticated and extended analysis than chronological time alone provides.

Utility of Policy Areas

The roles and influence of both the president and Congress vary considerably by policy areas, and all three typologies had at least some discriminating power. For a dichotomy, the two presidencies retains some utility. The recent decision by CQ to include an economic dimension, instead of just domestic and foreign, has been suggested by others (e.g., Manning 1977; LeLoup and Shull [1979a] 1991). Presidents do not appear to be more foreign policy oriented, taking relatively fewer positions in that domain. However, they do issue executive orders extensively in defense and in trade. Congress does appear more domestic oriented (in controversy measures) by challenging presidents relatively frequently in government and social welfare. Agriculture has such low salience that it probably should be subsumed with the other six areas, presumably mostly within resources. Although used only for important legislation, the Lowi typology, too, had utility. As expected, presidents seem more redistributive and constituent oriented and Congress more distributive and regulatory oriented. Implications of these policy typologies follow.

Two Presidencies Thesis
Although congressional influence in foreign policy does not yet match its power domestically, Congress is increasing its role considerably. The issue area where Congress has had the least influence has been in defense. Wars and crises in the twentieth century have led to substantial growth of presidential power. Yet even here Congress is asserting itself, particularly when presidents are thought to have exceeded their authority and encroached into areas where Congress also maintains constitutional responsibilities. Thus, while presiden-

tial powers have grown enormously, Congress appears to be catching up (Ripley and Lindsay 1993). There is no evidence, even when Congress and the president are of the same party, that this trend will reverse itself in the near future.

Reforms in budgeting and strengthened party leadership allow Congress a more equal role in all aspects of policy-making than occurred previously. Other efforts have given Congress a larger voice in military procurement, and reforms in committee assignments have provided more ideological balance on relevant committees, particularly Armed Services. Also, there is less perception of external threat (since the end of the Cold War) and a decreasing emphasis on military relative to diplomatic issues. Also, the globalization of the economy has further blurred differences between domestic and foreign policy. Still, Congress likely will continue to be more assertive in the domestic policy realm.

King and Ragsdale Categorization
Good evidence exists in this book that substantial variation in actor behavior occurs within domestic and foreign policy. However, showing that aid and trade differ dramatically in the foreign realm, and that social welfare and agriculture are quite different domestically, provides confidence that greater variation in behavior can be tapped than by using the dichotomy alone. The effort here simply combined trade, aid, and defense as categorized by these authors into the foreign dimension and social welfare (including civil rights), government (including economic management), resources, and agriculture into the domestic realm.[6] Although somewhat crude, the King and Ragsdale categorization incorporates some of both substantive and functional aspects of policy typologies.

The view that Congress dominates domestic and the president dominates foreign policy initiatives is too simplistic in both policy areas. Generally, Congress plays a lesser role in military intervention than in diplomacy or foreign aid. Congress tends not to be instrumental early in crisis or violent circumstances. Military secrecy and a presidential monopoly over the presentation of alternatives to Congress generally has minimized congressional scrutiny of national security strategy (Hinckley 1994). However, Congress has performed a greater role in budgetary and structural (military organization, training) issues of national security policy (Huntington 1961, 124). Obviously, Congress has asserted even greater influence in the domestic realm, particularly in issue areas like government and resource policies.

Lowi Typology
What can be concluded about the Lowi typology in examining presidential-congressional relations on votes on important legislation? First, the typology

revealed some dramatic changes in emphasis over time. The increasingly technical nature of society has necessitated a growth in *regulatory* policy.[7] This may have been largely at the expense of distributive issues, which dominated the policy arena in the nineteenth century (Lowi 1972, 300). Because of the level of expertise required, it is probable that a shift has occurred, moving policy-making generally and regulatory policy specifically from the legislative to the executive sphere (Vogler 1977, 304). Since *redistributive* issues tend to be controversial and ideological, normally it is the president, not Congress, who initiates policy in behalf of society's poor (Ripley and Franklin 1991, 148). Because it requires an assertive and committed president to initiate redistributive policies (Lowi 1972, 302–3), major change in such policies is least likely to be adopted.

Distributive policies are less ideological than regulatory and redistributive issues in that they involve fewer social rearrangements. Such issues as acreage allotments and water projects are more likely to be adopted by Congress than are the more conflictual redistributive policies (Ripley and Franklin 1991, 149; Hayes 1978, 154). *Constituent* policies often contain foreign policy content. Usually, they are developed centrally in both branches of government and are rather partisan. Sometimes they involve structural change, which may be a major area for independent presidential policy adoption through executive orders.

Assessment

Although all three policy typologies have discriminating value, none of the three is perfect. The two presidencies distinction appears less empirically obvious than it did in the 1960s. Yet, the phenomenon still exists, if more so for Republican than Democratic presidents. Although theory has been limited, considerable research has worked toward this end (Shull 1991, 1994; Lindsay and Steger 1993), and it is parsimonious. The King and Ragsdale categorization at first appears totally atheoretical, in that no rationale is provided for the issue area groupings. They are based loosely on two typologies identified empirically in early research, but the authors expanded on the foreign domain, as have others (Ripley and Franklin 1986, 1991; Shull et al. 1985; Lindsay and Ripley 1993, chap. 2; Hinckley 1994). Martha Gibson (1995) has provided the most theoretical development of the typology to date. The Lowi typology has the strongest theoretical foundation of the three but often has been difficult to apply empirically (Shull 1983; Spitzer 1983). All three typologies were used here, compiled within accepted limits of intercoder reliability, and found to have utility.

Tables 8.5 and 8.6 directly assess the political time and policy area groupings, generally finding neither consistently superior to the other. These

**TABLE 8.5. Comparing Ranges on Important
Legislation (by time and policy aggregations)**

Comparison	Position Taking	Controversy
Presidential party	6.8	7.5
Two presidencies	21.4	9.7
Presidents	12.3	34.4
King & Ragsdale	16.2	22.4
Year in term	9.5	14.5
Lowi	17.2	22.6

Note: Position taking refers to frequency per year in office. Controversy
is based on the mean vote split indicator.

tables compare the differences in ranges by time versus policy groupings to
anticipate which most differentiates government activities. Table 8.5 compares position taking and controversy on important legislation by year and
policy aggregations. It shows that for position taking, the two presidencies
thesis (policy aggregation) provides much greater differentiation than does
presidential party (time aggregation) and slightly more for controversy as
well. In comparing individual presidents and the King and Ragsdale typology,
table 8.5 shows that, despite having fewer observations (seven versus nine),
the latter differentiates position taking more, but the former differentiates
much better in measuring controversy (mean vote split). Finally, table 8.5

**TABLE 8.6. Comparing Ranges on All Legislation (by time
and policy aggregations)**

Comparison	Position Taking	Controversy	Support	Executive Orders
Presidential party	18.1	9.5	11.4	25.9
Two presidencies	36.2	3.6	3.6	11.1
Presidents	65.9	32.7	21.5	36.4[a]
King & Ragsdale	20.4	11.3	7.1	26.8[b]
Year in term	29.4	3.3	6.7	12.4

Note: Position taking refers to frequency per year in office. *Controversy* is based on the in- versus out-party
support indicator. *Support* refers to the average percentage agreement in the House with the presidents' vote
positions. *Executive orders* refers to the average number of executive orders issued per year.
    [a]Truman excluded from president ranges.
    [b]Other (nonpolicy) categories of executive orders excluded.

compares year in term with the Lowi typology, revealing the latter as considerably better at differentiating both activities on important legislation.

Table 8.6 makes similar comparisons for all legislation, where measures exist for each of the four government activities. The two presidencies thesis worked much better than presidential party only on position taking. On the other three indicators, presidential party provided superior differentiation. Although differences by the King and Ragsdale seven areas emerged, individual presidents (admittedly having two more observations than the policy categorization, nine versus seven) had greater ranges, so time did better than policy for each of the four government activities (see table 8.6). Differences by party were most dramatic on position taking and least on executive order issuance. Since no data were available for the Lowi typology on all legislation, selected years alone appear in table 8.6, showing greatest differentiation for position taking and least distinguishing value for vote controversy.

This chapter has summarized the findings and drawn implications from the research. Because it has been exploratory and broad ranging, no final decisions are warranted about the interrelationship of groupings of political time and policy areas in explaining relations between the president and Congress. Yet both revealed important differences in government activities. A multitude of variables and indicators are offered, and it should be quite clear to all that neither actor dominates the relationship. Perhaps now more than ever before, true power sharing best characterizes their interactions. The brief epilogue that follows lays out some specific future research strategies and assesses more generally the current and future state of presidential-congressional relations.

Epilogue: Directions for Presidential-Congressional Relations

This epilogue begins with suggested directions for future research. *Presidential-Congressional Relations* has introduced many variables in a preliminary fashion. As is usually the case with exploratory research, it suggests further avenues of inquiry. Scholars and students should learn from what has been uncovered here and utilize some of the concepts, variables, and data to further explore presidential-congressional relations. The ultimate goal should be explanation or even prediction, using whatever research enhances our understanding of the complex and multifaceted relationship between the president and Congress. The final section provides an overview of current and future prospects for presidential-congressional relations.

Future Research

Research on presidential-congressional relations in the 1950s and 1960s saw considerable presidential dominance, particularly in the realm of foreign policy (Rossiter 1956; Neustadt 1960; Wildavsky [1966] 1991). That view was challenged only slightly in the 1970s and 1980s (e.g., Edwards 1980; Shull 1983), but the 1990s brought a flurry of studies showing that Congress was not as submissive as had been portrayed previously. Although some researchers continue to see a limited role for Congress (Mezey 1989; Spitzer 1993; Hinckley 1994; Peterson 1994), others find very little evidence that presidents dominate the relationship (Bond and Fleisher 1990; Jones 1994, 1995; Ripley and Lindsay 1993). Although some researchers have gone too far with a counter view, the "tandem institutions" approach (Peterson 1990; LeLoup and Shull 1993; Thurber 1996) seems the most realistic way to view current interactions between Congress and presidents.

What should scholars consider in further examinations of presidential-congressional relations? One direction that clearly has not received enough attention is examining the relationships through public policy approaches, either through modeling the process or through content issue areas such as those included here. In addition, combining substantive and functional typologies should enhance theoretical and explanatory power. Future analysis is expected to amplify what has been observed here, namely, that neither presidents nor Congress act alone. Therefore, the relationship is one of tandem institutions sharing power rather than a dominant president or a submissive Congress.

It should be obvious to readers of this book that the analysis has been exploratory and conceptual. However, many variables and types of relationships have been introduced, some of which appear to have greater utility than others. Some of the relationships are suggestive of greater influence by presidents and others suggest greater influence by Congress, but the overall finding is one of the need for interaction, if not always full cooperation (LeLoup and Shull 1993). Neither branch can act alone and hope to accomplish very much. Subsequent scholars should incorporate many of these variables into their own research rather than study these actors in isolation or examine a single government activity.

Some current research incorporates sophisticated multivariate analysis. Widely cited studies (e.g., Bond and Fleisher 1990; Edwards 1989; Peterson 1990) utilize a single dependent variable, including minor variations of legislative support or success. Yet, neither of these variables nor any other indicator thereof (such as key votes or examining nonunanimous votes only)[1] tell the entire story of presidential-congressional relations. Presidential position taking, legislative vote controversy, executive order issuance, and phenomena not included here tell us much that support or success do not. Other venues, like legislative liaison and budgeting, need further scrutiny. Also, the political time and policy area groupings reveal sufficient variation to warrant further scrutiny.

Where do we go from here with research on presidential-congressional relations? Within Congress, scholars should consider committee voting and tracking the legislative history of bills to see if presidents can play a role. We need better ways of ascertaining whether bills (and their roll call votes) are part of the president's legislative agenda. That requires collecting the CQ box score (dropped in 1975) so that scholars are less dependent on presidents' vote positions for both the organization's current success and support scores. We need better data on the president's ability to shift votes in Congress, thereby tapping presidential leadership or influence rather than simple congruence of positions (Pritchard 1983; Sullivan 1991b; Mouw and MacKuen 1992). Improved measures of presidential success and failure with Congress, including explanations other than public support, would lead to better theory. Surely multivariate analysis is desirable. The National Science Foundation should help scholars improve data collection, storage, and dissemination much as it does for students of elections. Therefore, studying interactions between the first two branches of the national government more systematically is the most pressing problem for scholars of American political institutions.

Current/Anticipated Presidential-
Congressional Relations

Despite increased leadership powers such as central clearance and legislative liaison, conditions must be right for presidential leadership to be accepted. Generally, presidents who have cooperated with Congress have had greater success with their programs and, to a large measure, such cooperation is dependent upon the political climate. Presidents considered "strong" legislative leaders (e.g., Lyndon Johnson) had a partisan majority in Congress, while the presidents considered "weak" leaders over Congress (e.g., Gerald Ford) usually did not (LeLoup and Shull 1993, chap. 3). Although it may not be essential to have a large or even a simple partisan majority, a "philosophical" working majority helps presidents obtain their preferred policies. Assertive presidents seem to do better with Congress, and presidents who can advance their preferences with finesse likely will prosper. Certainly the notion of presidential dominance of the relationship has faded in recent years (Peterson 1990; Bond and Fleisher 1990; LeLoup and Shull 1993; Jones 1995).

Although Congress may be incapable of determining the nation's policy agenda by itself, it too can initiate policy. Congress is inclined toward initiation and innovation of its own in instances where a vacuum in presidential leadership exists. If the president who would initiate policy is encouraged to cooperate with Congress that body too is most effective in collaboration with a strong president. Congress has strengthened its hand in many ways since executive abuses during Vietnam and Watergate. It seems highly unlikely today that presidents could run roughshod over Congress like Johnson did in 1967 with the Gulf of Tonkin Resolution. For every increase in presidential leadership powers, seemingly, corresponding congressional checks exist (Ripley and Lindsay 1993).

This revisionist position asserts that presidential dominance is far too simplistic a picture of policy-making and suggests a much more independent role for Congress relative to the president. Studies countering the presidential dominant view contend that congressional deficiencies in policy development are not irreversible and argue that Congress, rather than being restrained by legal or constitutional restrictions, basically lacks the will to challenge presidents effectively. While some observers feel Congress must exert itself if presidential prerogatives (and also presidential abuses) are to be held in check, they are not very optimistic (Spitzer 1993; Mezey 1989), especially in foreign policy (Peterson 1994; Hinckley 1994). However, critics of the presidential dominant literature generally see congressional initiative as the only hope for such a counterbalance.

Despite numerous reassertions of its constitutional and oversight powers, Congress generally has had difficulty performing a leadership role in foreign policy-making. The gap between its formal powers and actual influence has been considerable, but it has opportunities for initiative in both diplomatic and military aspects of foreign policy. Examples where the legislature's role may be substantial include foreign trade, aid, and immigration legislation.[2] Although the president may originate a proposal, Congress frequently takes over with substantial modification. Certainly Congress is preeminent in policy adoption, and even presidential issuance of executive orders is related to its support in the legislative environment. Congress has had a much greater role in foreign policy development since the late 1960s.[3] It has initiated in such areas as the SALT Treaty and restricting the CIA, limiting presidential power to commit troops and act in emergency situations, and modifying presidential policies such as détente, arms sales, and treaties.

Presidential influence in congressional voting is limited, particularly in domestic policy. In turn, many factors affect congressional support for presidents' legislative positions and the success of their policy initiatives. For example, the president usually fares better when he utilizes congressional leaders in policy formulation. Presidential leadership over Congress is increasingly difficult in the domestic realm, however, as conflict rather than cooperation is more the norm in recent years, especially in such issue areas as social welfare and agriculture. Conflict over floor voting can disrupt presidential preferences, and efforts to minimize such conflict are largely out of the presidents' hands. The legislative environment itself greatly influences interactions between Congress and the president (Edwards 1989; Bond and Fleisher 1990).

His first two years in office (1993–94) revealed Bill Clinton as having greater average success in Congress than nearly any modern president, winning his way on 86.4 percent of his vote positions in both chambers (*CQ Weekly Reports,* January 27, 1996, 194). Clinton appeared to be in the catbird seat. But if the 1994 congressional elections proved anything, it is that political fortunes are fleeting, and policy change is both unpredictable and inevitable. The 104th Congress beginning in January 1995 was a very different one from the 103rd. Republicans won elections extensively and took control of both chambers in Congress. Clinton's legislative success in 1995 plummeted to the lowest level in history to just 36.2 percent. Congress was newly invigorated, largely taking over the public policy agenda.

This legislative dominance was unprecedented in modern times, but by the end of 1995, Clinton was more popular than House Speaker Newt Gingrich, and little of the conservative agenda in the Contract for America had been adopted. Only 88 bills had been signed into law, the lowest number since 1933. Partisan rancor intensified, averaging a record high of 70 percent of partisan votes in both chambers (*CQ Weekly Reports,* January 27, 1996, 196,

199). And despite exceedingly low support from Congress in 1995, a very partisan Republican Congress passed the line-item veto when a Democrat was president (even though it did not take effect until January 1997).[4] However, even this very limited (possibly unconstitutional) action signals a capitulation by Congress of its considerable constitutional power of the purse. Supporters of an independent legislature feared a return to presidential dominance of the relationship that had grown more equal in power sharing.

During 1996, Clinton doubled his legislative support in the House to 53 percent approval and his legislative success improved dramatically to 55.1 percent from its lowest figure in history during 1995. The 18.9 percent increase was also a historical high but not all that impressive for fourth-year presidents (All Politics, "CQ's Presidential Support," January 5, 1997, 1). Still, as CQ stated, "By the end of the session, Clinton had clearly gained the upper hand" (3). Partisanship in voting also decreased considerably from the 1995 levels, especially in the House. Indeed, Republican support for Clinton's vote positions increased substantially in this single year.

Clinton won reelection handily in 1996 over Bob Dole, the only successful presidential nominee in many years running directly from a congressional leadership position. Dole may have run a lackluster campaign, but he may also have suffered in part from voters who continued to punish Congress more than presidents for the country's woes. Dole's Senate had been much more moderate than Gingrich's House in pushing the conservative agenda, and fewer Republican senators were defeated for reelection. Indeed, the Republicans gained two Senate seats but lost eight House seats. Thus, the GOP majority in the House had overplayed its hand.

The contentious 1996 election was actually preceded by considerable presidential-congressional cooperation, much of which was not always evident during the rancor of the election. For example, Clinton's primary goal of that year was welfare reform and Public Law 104-193 passed with bipartisan support after several false starts and compromises. Many other major issues passed that year as a result of compromise (e.g., increasing the minimum wage, revising telecommunications laws, and granting most favored national status to China). The public may have wanted divided government but it also wanted less fighting and both the White House and Congress appeared to move toward the political center. The electorate made it clear that it was watching both branches (the leaders of each were wounded by ethics scandals) and that it expected results.

What do these developments portend for the future of presidential-congressional relations? Deadlock and policy gridlock could occur but it is hoped that greater respect and accommodation between these vital institutions will result. As is often the case, this drive toward the ideological center and mutual accommodation resulted more from political weakness than from strength. Both branches seemed to recognize that only by cooperating, rather than through conflict, would the policy goals of either be accomplished. Renewed efforts toward compromise and policy agreement should enhance governability as America enters the twenty-first century.

Appendixes

Classification of Important Legislation

This appendix shows how the Barbara Hinckley data on important legislation were adapted to David Mayhew's (1992) and how the votes were classified into policy areas. Hinckley's (1994) operationalization of important legislation is added to Mayhew's important legislation in order to increase the number of votes on important legislation overall and, particularly, in the foreign policy dimension. One disadvantage, however, is that important legislation is determined slightly differently by the two authors. Hinckley provides a sparse two paragraphs defining such legislation. Her criteria are that it "must be a) brought to a vote on the floor of at least one chamber, and b) featured in *Congressional Quarterly Almanac*'s annual review of foreign policy" (1994, 205). She goes on to state that "the list thus excludes from the larger working agenda routine extensions of programs, minor programs, or specific changes or provisions when these are not related to major issues of the day." Hinckley includes executive agreements but they are deleted from this important legislation data set. Finally, unlike Mayhew, Hinckley's major "legislation" need not have passed, so any votes that failed adoption are eliminated.

The Mayhew/Hinckley important legislation was then categorized according to the King and Ragsdale seven categories (see table A.1). (Recall that the King and Ragsdale groupings also form the basis for the two presidencies substantive typology.) Beginning with Mayhew, Hinckley's data were added, leaving out any duplicates to eliminate double counting. The frequency counts of these two data sets were kept separate so that they can be collapsed or combined as desired (see tables 3.1 and 3.2). Two independent coders obtained an intercoder reliability of 91 percent agreement for the Mayhew and 95 percent agreement for the Hinckley data into the King and Ragsdale typology. Differences were resolved with confidence that roll calls can be coded reliably into these categories. The King and Ragsdale definitions (1988, 72) for each category with my expansion (which is used for all votes as well) appear in table A.1.

Next, the Mayhew/Hinckley important legislation vote data were categorized into the Theodore Lowi functional typology. A comparable table A.2 lists the various substantive issues that were coded as fitting into the Lowi typology. Admittedly, some issues do not fit as easily as they did into the

TABLE A.1. Coding the King and Ragsdale Typology

This data set categorizes roll calls collected for the Mayhew/Hinckley important legislation according to the King and Ragsdale categories used for all roll call votes in the House of Representatives. King and Ragsdale provide too few guidelines for reliably coding substantive issues, so I expanded upon their definitions considerably. Differences were resolved with confidence that roll calls can be placed reliably into these categories. The King and Ragsdale definitions (1988, 72) for each category with my expansion follow.

foreign trade = diplomacy, immigration, trade; Shull's expansion: import/export, executive/international agreements unless otherwise specified, sanctions, tariff, diplomacy (e.g., country recognition), Panama Canal

foreign aid = foreign aid; Shull's expansion: any international aid when not defense; includes State Department, USIA, Peace Corps, IMF, UN, USIA

defense = military, veterans; Shull's expansion: Department of Defense, NASA, space, nuclear, draft, intelligence, communism (e.g., Radio Free Europe), Cuba, disarmament, arms sales except if restricted to trade/aid; peacekeeping, mutual security

social welfare = social welfare, Indian rights, civil rights, education; Shull's expansion: health, medical schools, homeless, disabilities, minimum wage, unemployment, job training, food stamps, but not social security, voting rights

government/economic management = government management, economy, taxation; Shull's expansion: civil service, reorganization (except DOD), social security, retirement, union laws, lending, communications, public broadcasting, statehood, campaign laws

resources = energy, national resources, environment, transportation; Shull's expansion: crime, gun control, housing, drugs, energy (except nuclear), consumer stability, forest management, reclamation, urban development, federal resources to states

agriculture = agriculture, farm; Shull's expansion: food additives, Appalachian development, poultry, commodity subsidies, food aid

---

TABLE A.2. Coding the Lowi Typology

Distributive (D)	Regulatory (G)	Redistributive (R)	Constituent (C)
Grants, loans, contracts, construction (health, education, space, military)	Natural Resources (land use, strip mining, environment, energy controls)	Welfare, poverty, almost all civil rights (voting, public accommodations, busing, desegregation age, sex, race)	National security and space (when not research and development) Communism
Public works (water projects, parks, recreation)	Regulating, transportation, atomic power, food and drug	American Indians	Civil defense DOD
Agriculture (most issues including subsidies)	Trade (imports and exports, customs) Rhodesia/South Africa	Unemployment, minimum wage, labor benefits, public housing, rent control	Treaties Atomic Weapons/ Control

(Continued)

TABLE A.2.—*Continued*

Distributive (D)	Regulatory (G)	Redistributive (R)	Constituent (C)
Soil conservation	Most economic issues (antitrust, oil prices)	Social Security	Military assistance Intelligence
Research and development (space, atomic, transportation, all training programs)	Labor restrictions, general taxation	Medicare, Medicaid	Civil service (pay raises, awards, federal employment)
Federalism issues	Crime and internal security	Taxation (when changes in burdens), IMF	Selective Service, draft
Area redevelopment	Consumer protection	Foreign economic aid World Bank	Presidential disability
Impacted aid (aid to cities/states)	Election reform	Immigration (quotas, refugees), UN	District of Columbia
Government services	Pollution, smoking laws, radiation control	Famine relief Peace Corps	Reorganization, restructuring, overhead
National Parks	General rules, controls, reforms	Food stamps, Food for Peace, State Dept.	Executive authority, "administrative" pres., clarifying procedures
Post Office	Budget/deficit	Urban renewal	Statehood: modernize or amend existing laws/ facilities, any modernization
Veterans benefits			Propaganda, any communications pol., reapportionment
Revenue sharing Provide insurance			New agency

substantive typology. As reiterated elsewhere, foreign issues are especially difficult to include there since Lowi (1964, 1972), Robert Spitzer (1983), and Steven Shull (1983) gave this issue area little attention. Randall Ripley and Grace Franklin's (1991) work helps in this regard, but the task is still difficult. Using the chart in table A.2, an independent coder and I were able to reach an intercoder reliability score on the Lowi typology of .89 for the Mayhew and .88 for the Hinckley data. Although slightly less reliable than for the King and Ragsdale typology, intercoder reliability is still within acceptable limits (Gurr 1972).

Codebooks

Appendix B provides codebooks for the various categorizations of votes on important and all legislation. Table B.1 is for important legislation. Harry Truman is included in V4 because some executive order data are available for him. Divided government (V6) and the year in presidential term (V7) show all years for which at least some data exist. V7 also provides more refinement for important legislation than for all legislation because the CQ vote information is available on a monthly basis.

Table B.2 provides a codebook for the all legislation data, which are collected on a slightly different basis but generally are comparable to important legislation. Note that for all legislation, the year is the unit of analysis, and the individual information for each vote is not incorporated. This all-legislation data set also contains information about presidents, such as their ideology and popular support on a yearly basis, but this information is not presented in this volume.

TABLE B.1. Codebook for Votes on Important Legislation

Number	Variable	Column	Value	
V1	Cumulative	1–3	001–999	
V2	Year	5–6	47–95	
V3	Month	7–8	01 = Jan. . . . 12 = Dec.	
V4	President	9–10	1	HST
			2	DDE
			3	JFK
			4	LBJ
			5	RMN
			6	GRF
			7	JEC
			8	RWR
			9	GHWB
			10	WJC
V5	President's party	11	1	Democrat
			2	Republican

(*continued*)

Number	Variable	Column	Value		
V6	Party government[a]	12	1	Divided = 47–48, 55–60, 69–76, 81–92, 95	
			2	Unified = 49–54, 61–68, 77–80, 93–94	
V7	Year in pres. term[b]	13	1	First = 53, 61, 64 (11/63–4/64), 69, 74 (8–12), 75, 77, 81, 89, 93	
			2	Last = 52, 60, 68, 88, (Jan. 61, 69, 77, 81, 89, 93)	
			3	Reelection = 48, 56, 64 (5–12) 72, 76, 80, 84, 92	
			4	Other = (residual), 74 (1–7)	
V8	K & R policy areas	14	1	Foreign trade (TR)	
			2	Foreign Aid (AI)	
			3	Defenses (DF)	
			4	Social welfare (SW)	
			5	Government (GO)	
			6	Resources (RE)	
			7	Agriculture (AG)	
V9	Lowi typology	15	1	Distributive (D)	
			2	Regulatory (G)	
			3	Redistributive (R)	
			4	Constituent (C)	
V10	# Amendments	17–18	1–99		
V11	Chamber	19	1	House	
			2	Senate	
V12	Pres. position	20	1	Yes	
			2	No	
V13	Legislative support	21	1	Yes	
			2	No	
V14	Party vote (50% D vote against 50% R)	22	1	Yes	
			2	No	
V15	CQ #	24–26	1–999		
V16	Source of data	27	1	Mayhew	
			2	Hinckley	
			3	CQ generally (K&R) all	
V17	# voting yes	28–30	0–435		
V18	# voting no	31–33	0–435		
V19	Type passage[c]	34	1	Voice	
			2	Roll Call	
V20	Mean vote split[d]	35–37	0–100		
V21	Nonunanimous votes[e]	38–40	0–100		

[a]Divided government years include some years not analyzed here.

[b]Year-in-presidential-term include some years not analyzed here, but for the years in this study (1957–1994), the *N*s are as follows: first = 9.1; last = 3.6; reelection = 5.8; and other = 23.5.

[c]The data for voice votes incorporate V1–V12 from this codebook.

[d]The calculation is yeas − nays divided by total substracted from 1.0 (see chap. 5).

[e]Percentage of votes where margin of passage is closer than 80 percent yeas and 20 percent nays or vice versa.

TABLE B.2. Codebook for All Vote Data and Executive Orders

Number	Variable	Value
	Calendar year	1947–94
	Value labels for president	1 = HST
		2 = DDE
		3 = JFK
		4 = LBJ
		5 = RMN
		6 = GRF
		7 = JEC
		8 = RWR
		9 = GHWB
		10 = WJC
1	Executive Orders (all)	
2	EO-trade	
3	EO-aid	
4	EO-defense	
5	EO-social welfare/civil rights	
6	EO-government/economic management	
7	EO-resources	
8	EO-agriculture	
9	EO-ceremonial/cultural	
10	EO-federalism	
11	EO-personal/agency requests	
12	average number members of Congress from president's party	
13	presidential vote positions as percentage of all roll call votes	
14	position taking trade	
15	position taking aid	
16	position taking defense	
17	position taking social welfare	
18	position taking government	
19	position taking national resources	
20	position taking agriculture	
21	legislative support of the president in the House (overall)	
22	legislative support trade	
23	legislative support aid	
24	legislative support defense	
25	legislative support social welfare	
26	legislative support government	
27	legislative support resources	
28	legislative support agriculture	
29	number of veto challenges	
30	year in presidential term of office	(1–8)

(*continued*)

Number	Variable	Value
31	presidential party	1 = Democrat
		0 = Republican
32	presidential liberalism (ADA)	
33	number pages in the *Federal Register*	
34	number employees in Executive Office of the President	
35	average popular support (Gallup percentage who approve)	
36	year in term of office	1 = first
		2 = last
		3 = reelection
		4 = other
37	type government	1 = divided
		2 = unified
38	in party support of the president	1 = trade
		2 = aid
		3 = defense
		4 = social welfare
		5 = government
		6 = resources
		7 = agriculture
39	out party support of the president	1 = trade
		2 = aid
		3 = defense
		4 = social welfare
		5 = government
		6 = resources
		7 = agriculture

Notes

Chapter 1

1. Those areas of congressional influence in domestic policy initiation have been identified by Sundquist 1968, 535; Gallagher 1977; Jones 1984; Chamberlain 1946; Price 1972; Moe and Teel 1970.

2. Measures of Congress's propensity for policy initiation could include the number of presidential veto override attempts and actual overrides, total number of bills enacted, percentage of the presidents' requests or positions on legislative votes approved, number of reports required of the executive, congressional investigations, and subpoena of executive witnesses.

3. The Senate, as the more liberal body in the 1960s and 1970s, generally was more assertive in social policy innovation than was the House (Polsby 1969, 65; 1975, 229). The Senate had become more conservative by the 1980s.

4. Exceptions to presidential initiative in the post–World War II era include Democratic Congresses in the 1950s and 1970s under Eisenhower and Nixon/Ford and the Republican Congress in 1995–96, particularly the House with Speaker Newt Gingrich and the Republican Contract With America.

5. Those arguing for presidential dominance in foreign policy include Dahl 1950; Koenig 1975; Robinson 1967; Donovan 1974; Clausen 1973; Destler 1974, 85. However, early studies countering that Congress has an important foreign policy role include Orfield 1975; Gallagher 1977; Chamberlain 1946; Sundquist 1968; Moe and Teel 1970; Johannes 1972a; 1972b; Fisher 1972.

6. Lowi seems to view redistributive policies as allocating resources from the rich to the poor, but others show that such policies could have the opposite effect, that is, from poor to rich (Vogler 1977; Hayes 1978).

7. Chapter 3 shows that supporting the president's positions on roll call votes need not actually lead to the adoption of policy. Amendments and other votes may occur before final passage.

8. Although it would also be interesting to dichotomize these data by divided and unified government, the values are identical to presidential party for the years examined (except executive orders, which include Truman). In other words, from 1957 to 1994, Republicans always had divided and Democratic presidents always had unified government by the strict definition.

Chapter 2

1. Examples of congressional frustration of presidential preferences in foreign policy since Wildavsky wrote include the following: Johnson on foreign aid and

military assistance, Nixon on aid authorizations and the Pentagon Papers, Ford on aid to Southeast Asia and African development, Carter on the Salt II treaty, Reagan on arms sales and aid to the Contras, Bush on his Secretary of Defense nominee, and Clinton initially on his proposed intervention in Bosnia.

2. A multiple-presidencies approach may help build bridges between substantive and functional content areas of public policy. Obviously, both the King and Ragsdale typology and the Lowi typology are multiple, while the two presidencies is dichotomous.

3. Spitzer falsely assumes that perception of a policy's purpose, not the purpose itself, influences behavior. If behavior is the dependent variable, then the actor's perception of the statute's purpose is the independent variable. Therefore, policy type should be operationalized on the basis of perceived purpose, not original intent. An additional consideration is that there will always be cases that are difficult to operationalize because they can fall into more than one policy area. This problem of ambiguity may not have a satisfactory solution. However, the problem can be avoided by distinguishing between Spitzer's "pure" and "mixed" cases (1983, 29–31). If only pure cases are used as data, then the testing of hypotheses will not be biased by the difficulties resulting from the attempt to classify mixed cases.

4. An examination of the figures provided throughout Shull's 1983 book appears to indicate the existence of differing degrees of ordinal continuity between substantive policy types across environmental conditions.

5. Because Spitzer only offers a graphical interpretation, it is difficult to determine if policy patterns are consistent over time. He could solve this problem by generating a correlation matrix for each policy area based on presidential term cycles.

Chapter 3

1. Subsequent variations of the box score that incorporate innovative approximations of presidential agenda preferences appear in Light (1982) and Peterson (1990).

2. Greater focus on the individual members of Congress as well as on Congress as an institution is desirable. Such an approach requires more work, but it offers the opportunity to use creative independent variables. Of course, the problem with this strategy is identifying initial positions and isolating presidential influence from all the other influences that have an effect on how members of Congress vote. Whatever the problems, both individual-level analysis (including the roll call itself as a unit of analysis) and aggregate analysis, used here, are important for understanding presidential-congressional relations.

3. An example occurs with King and Ragsdale's categorization of presidential vetoes. Few cases occur for some policy areas (e.g., none for foreign aid from 1957–84). Obviously, it would be difficult to compare veto issuance across the seven policy categories, let alone the even more infrequent veto challenges or overrides. Fewer problems occur with roll call votes, but some individual year Ns are limited.

4. This observation was made by Mayhew to the author in September 1995.

5. Goldfinger and Shull (1995) argue that divided government should be examined

as a continuum of party margins in Congress rather than as purely dichotomous unified or divided.

6. Unfortunately, when examining selected years, the data points are few, especially for last (lame-duck) year, which equals just three cases (1960, 1968, 1988). Because votes on important legislation are dated by month, that allows the addition of the following as last years: January of 1961, 1969, 1977, 1981, 1989, and 1993.

7. For important legislation, 1963 is treated as a Kennedy year and November 1963–April 1964 as the first Johnson year. The 1974 case is weighted to reflect the relative time served by Nixon and Ford in that year (Nixon = January–July; Ford = August–December, which is the latter's first year). The year 1968 is considered a last year because Johnson announced early on that he would not run for reelection. Because of this circumstance, Johnson's reelection year = May–December 1964.

8. Shull (1989, 94) found fewer executive orders in civil rights issued on average during last than during first or reelection years. Presumably, presidents use them to set the stage in agenda setting rather than when they exit the stage.

9. It has already been seen that important and all legislation cannot be compared on legislative support of the president.

10. Appendix A provides the classification of important legislation. Note in the table how duplication was avoided and how nonlegislation (such as executive agreements) and bills that did not pass were dropped from the Hinckley data set. The data sets were kept separate for this analysis, but they can also be combined to average 16.2 roll call votes on final passage of important legislation per year. This rather small number, especially when grouped by policy area, makes yearly analysis problematic. However, the small N problem is of less concern here because the groupings of political time offer many more votes in each category.

11. A not surprising prelude to this notion is that roll call votes appear most often on average under the controversial Ford administration, an "activist mood" period according to Mayhew (1992). The fewest average number of votes on controversial legislation occur under the seemingly not very controversial Eisenhower administration and under Bush, whose administration is expected to be quite controversial in the legislative arena. In short, the data presented suggest but do not establish, particularly by individual president and by selected year in their term of office, controversy due to number of roll call votes on important legislation.

12. Hinckley's data probably would constitute an even higher percentage of foreign votes were it not for the fact that her votes that overlapped with Mayhew's were dropped.

Chapter 4

1. Such percentages by issue area are as a percentage of total positions taken. Since Ragsdale (1996) does not provide the votes themselves categorized by issue area, caution must be exercised in interpreting these percentages due to the differing number of votes by issue area for any given year. Because the number of votes each year is so variable, percentages of position taking by issue area and political time are more valuable than are proportions by the number of votes available.

2. George Edwards, Andrew Barrett, and Jeffrey Peake (1997) observe that presidents take positions on important legislation three times more often during divided than during unified government. The authors find that position taking is also high on important bills that failed to pass from 1947 to 1992. Thus, during divided government, presidents are able to prevent much legislation they oppose.

3. Presidential positions on voice votes are not identified by CQ. Some final passage bills are voice votes rather than recorded votes. A discussion of these voice votes appears in chapter 5.

4. As discussed in chapter 3, Ragsdale provides the data on position taking by issue area for the House only.

5. Such a number is not as small as it first appears because only about eight important laws pass Congress each year, so most of those are on roll calls on which the president took a position. Obviously, position taking counts twice on each important law if it passes both chambers with the president having taken a roll call vote position in each chamber.

6. This latter finding seems surprising given that presidents could be expected to appeal to rural constituencies more during reelection years.

7. The finding of greater attention to redistributive and less attention to distributive policies might seem risky as a presidential strategy, but the latter is observed in chapter 5 on several measures to be as controversial as the former.

Chapter 5

1. CQ defines the conservative coalition as "a voting bloc in the House and Senate consisting of a majority of Republicans and a majority of Southern Democrats, combined against a majority of Northern Democrats" (*Congressional Roll Call 1994* 1995, 9c).

2. CQ for a long period reported the particular roll call votes used to identify the ideological ratings of legislators from four different organizations in both their *Almanac* and *Congressional Roll Call* volumes. Regrettably, they stopped reporting these after 1991, so no basis for a presidential ADA score exists. Scholars must contact such organizations directly to find the particular votes used for rankings, and then a presidential score can be calculated according to whether presidents took positions on votes favoring or opposing the organizations (Gomez and Shull 1995). CQ reports individual legislator scores today only in its *Who's Who in Congress*.

3. The correlation between presidential party and their ADA score for the years covered here is $r = .835$.

4. We considered constructing an index for these measures of controversy, but none are correlated greater than .30 so they clearly tap different dimensions. Controversy is a continuum, and the various indicators are not simply additive.

5. The *Congressional Quarterly Almanac* provides data on whether the legislation was passed by voice or roll call vote and also the number of related amendments. Votes on "final" passage require some explanation. The focus is on the chamber approval of legislation. As indicated, most such approvals are roll call votes, particularly in recent years as opposed to the earlier years of the study. However, voice votes occasionally appear on final passage but more frequently when the chamber is confirming a confer-

ence committee recommendation. In this sense, voting on conference committee reports is similar to omnibus appropriations in that much of the controversy has already been resolved. Thus, the concern here is on chamber passage even if "final" passage after a conference report is sometimes very routine. In order for the voice votes variable to reflect controversy, the proportion of non–voice votes is used; for example, the greater the proportion of non–voice votes, the greater the controversy.

6. Obviously, variation occurs within presidents' terms. For example, Reagan obtained greater support from the opposition party during his first term than during his second. Also, Democrats regained control of the Senate during his last two years in office (1987–88).

7. Gibson (1995) compares in- versus out-party support for presidents according to the King and Ragsdale (1988) groupings.

8. See Shaw and Shull (1996) for a multivariate test of determinants of vote controversy on important legislation.

Chapter 6

1. It is unclear what source CQ used prior to the publication of the *Weekly Compilation of Presidential Documents* in 1965, but in a letter to the author, Research Director Robert Cuthrell presumed that *Public Papers* and other documents were sources for initiatives. Nevertheless, it was CQ's judgment whether an issue mentioned in a presidential message constituted an actual legislative request. If more than one presidential remark was directed toward the issue, only the most definitive statement was used to track through the legislative process.

2. This charge is not totally accurate since most major requests appear in the form of multiple initiatives (Shull and LeLoup [1981] 1991). The box score of presidential initiatives are simply calls for legislation, not necessarily actual legislation before Congress. Thus, they show whether the president follows through on his stated agenda preferences but do not assure us that the request was actually introduced in Congress.

3. A massive data collection project on the box score throughout history is currently underway. Interested readers should contact Michael Malbin at State University of New York (Albany).

4. CQ began collecting support in 1953 but changed the coding rules so data from 1953–56 are not exactly equivalent to later data (Ragsdale 1996, 382). Besides, it did not code them according to easily identifiable policy categories in the four earlier years.

5. This finding on overall legislative support of vote positions corresponds with Kennedy's lack of success on his civil rights legislative requests (CQ's box score measure). Only 5 percent were approved, by far the lowest legislative success of any president on their civil rights initiatives to Congress (Shull 1989, 116). Ford took not a single position on a civil rights vote and, therefore, could have no support.

6. I would like to thank Johnny Goldfinger for helpful suggestions in this and the next section.

7. CQ changed the method of calculating individual member scores in 1987. Prior to that time, it used as the basis the total number of votes, regardless of whether a member was present. Beginning in that year, they also provide a separate score that discounts for absences. The newer score thus assumes that member percentage support

and opposition add up to 100 percent (*Almanac* 1987, 22-C). The change in calculating individual legislator scores does not affect the overall average percentage support measure used here.

8. Although CQ's most recent success and support scores are both based upon presidential position taking, the results can be quite different. For example, Clinton's overall success in 1994 was 87.4 percent while his overall support in the House was just 61.2 percent. These scores were more comparable in 1995 at 26.3 percent and 36.2 percent, respectively. His success varied by issue area (30 percent in defense and foreign policy, 28 percent in domestic policy, and 13 percent in economic policy and trade; *CQ Weekly Reports,* January 27, 1996, 237). In 1996 Clinton's success and support increased dramatically to 55.1 percent and 58 percent respectively (All Politics, "Presidential Support Definitions," December 27, 1996, 1).

9. Recall that Edwards, Barrett, and Peake (1997) examine important legislation that did not pass, and one could collect all roll calls on both those that did and did not pass for a more inclusive data set for future analysis than that offered here.

10. Because the scores reported are aggregations (means of means of Ragsdale's yearly percentages), some bias may appear. Also, the data seemingly contain some inaccuracies (e.g., Clinton took two positions on agriculture votes in 1993; Ragsdale 1996, table 8.6), but no agriculture support score is presented for him because, presumably, no positions were taken (Ragsdale 1996, table 8.10).

11. As mentioned previously, the number of data points are few for Ford and Clinton, because of limited years, so caution is urged in interpreting these individual president comparisons.

12. Recall that Reagan's Republican Party had control over the Senate during six of his eight years in office, but King and Ragsdale do not provide Senate votes at all, let alone individual votes designated by issue area. Presumably, Reagan had higher proportions of Senators than House members supporting his vote positions during those years.

13. Recall that neither success nor support measure the passage of legislation. For example, Clinton's high marks in 1994 belie the failure of his number-one priority (health care) even to make it to the floor of Congress. At the same time, his very low scores in 1995 mask the fact that he succeeded in preventing much Republican legislation from being enacted into law. Congress overrode only one of his eleven vetoes that year (he issued none during 1993–94). In the end, Republicans even gave up on their proposal to balance the federal budget in seven years (*CQ Weekly Reports,* January 27, 1996, 213). During 1996, none of Clinton's six vetoes were overturned, his support scores improved, and Congress passed legislation he had pushed on the minimum wage, safe drinking water, defense authorizations, and other measures.

Chapter 7

1. Although Allison's work is based upon decision making during the Cuban missile crisis, it is not purely a case study since he posits three models as potential explanations for the decision: rational actor, organizational behavior, and bureaucratic politics, the latter of which he gives greatest credence.

2. Some confusion exists over the distinction among executive orders, memoranda, and proclamations. The former are numbered and are more public than directed at private parties. However, no legal distinction among them exists (Utter and Cooper 1995, 4–5).

3. These terms, *adoption* and *implementation*, are incorporated frequently in models of the policy-making process. See Jones (1984) for a classic description and Shull and Gleiber (1994) for an empirical test of such a process.

4. Later research should examine whether executive orders may be seen in terms of adoption, implementation, or administration. They may relate to three additional concepts (activity, demands, and autonomy) tentatively posited. *Activity* refers to the president's desire for assertiveness, which may be largely related to personality and predispositions (Barber 1992). Personal preferences are also important but are not exercised in isolation; rather, they depend upon resources and constraints evident in the president's external environments. *Autonomy* is the traditional assumption that as chief executive, presidents "control" implementation and operate in the executive or administrative environment with few limitations. Research is divided over whether presidents influence the executive branch (Moe 1982; Wood and Anderson 1993; Wood and Waterman 1991) or whether bureaucrats have considerable discretion from presidential influence (Garand and Gross 1982; Eisner and Meier 1990; Shull and Garland 1996). Finally, as chief legislators, presidents are often influential actors within the legislative system. Conversely, *demands* from Congress constrain even seemingly administrative activities by presidents.

5. These authors observe a positive correlation (r = .485) between presidents' legislative support and their executive order issuance.

6. All further evaluations of executive order issuance by type of government differed so minutely from presidential party that the distinction is dropped from further analysis. Some argue that a dichotomous variable of divided government has limited discriminating power (see Goldfinger and Shull 1995). Certainly different states of divided government may exist, such as when Reagan had a Republican Senate but a Democratic House.

7. Surprisingly, Clinton's order issuance frequency changed little after 1994 with Republican control of Congress.

8. Note in all the two presidencies tables that the overall *N*s are not the same as for the Ragsdale (1996) data because the former omits the other (nonsubstantive) category.

9. An example of the former is Clinton's foreign disaster assistance executive order No. 12966 on July 14, 1995.

10. Recall from chapter 6 that social welfare was also the issue area of greatest party difference in legislative support of the presidents' vote positions.

11. Readers should recall that just two years' worth of data for Ford and Clinton warrant caution in interpreting this finding.

Chapter 8

1. The rank orderings presented in tables 8.1 through 8.4 are seemingly simple but can be confusing. They should be interpreted so that the lowest number represents the highest rank. For example, a 1 reflects greatest average position taking, but least mean

controversy, greatest mean support, and highest average executive order issuance. Any higher number reflects less salience (e.g., lower support). Thus, the lower number reflects greater activity but also lower controversy over vote positions.

2. The roll call data are available through the Inter-University Consortium for Political and Social Research (ICPSR) at the University of Michigan.

3. An example of such usage is the following terminology: "*success* in legislative struggles spanning more than one session in a Congress is not recorded in the Box-score" (*Almanac* 1973, 99, my emphasis).

4. At the time this book went to press, Ragsdale was attempting to gather these data. I have encouraged her to include them in the next edition of her invaluable book.

5. Grouping data by year in presidential term may also produce some measurement error. Part of the problem no doubt results from the widely differing years available; just three "last" years met the strict definition for all legislation. Alternatively, "other" years had by far the most observations, leading to the conclusion that the selected year distinction is not as useful as had been hoped. Having the important legislation roll call data by date allowed some expansion, such as utilizing the month of January for several presidents who were leaving office due to reelection defeat or being a lame duck. Those months added cases to last years for important legislation.

6. Some danger occurs in grouping domestic and foreign as King and Ragsdale do (1988, 53). For example, they include immigration with foreign trade, while other authors (beginning with Wildavsky [1966] 1991) recognize that immigration contains elements of foreign, domestic, and economic policy.

7. The *National Journal* documents a tremendous surge of regulation beginning about 1970. Nearly half of the federal regulatory agencies have been established since then, and the number of pages in the *Federal Register* more than tripled by 1980 (*Federal Register*, January 19, 1980, 101). However, 1980 was the highest on record (87,012), dropping particularly under Reagan, and then leveling off since to 68,108 pages in 1994 (Ornstein et al. 1996, 165).

Epilogue

1. The observant reader may wonder why the important legislation subset of roll call votes is incorporated but the key votes subset of all votes is not. Chapter 6 revealed that key votes have their uses but tap some concepts better than others. For example, key votes measure congruence of preferences well in terms of support but do not get at final passage at all. If one used just the key votes subset, very few observations would remain, especially when grouped into policy areas or political time.

2. An example of the latter is the 1986 Immigration Reform Act. It reflects the kind of issue on which Congress often leads; those that take a long time to percolate. LeLoup and Shull discuss this legislation revealing congressional leadership on an issue area that was not highly salient to most legislators or their constituents (1993, 132–35).

3. Numerous authors cover the resurgence of Congress in foreign policy in the late 1960s and early 1970s (Manley 1971, 61; Laurance 1976; Fisher 1972, 236; Schwarz and Shaw, 1976, 313). More contemporary examinations include LeLoup and Shull

1993, chap. 5; Ripley and Lindsay 1993; Hinckley 1994; Peterson 1994; and Thurber 1996.

4. Like all recent presidents, Clinton had long favored the line-item veto, even when his partisans were in control of Congress. As a former governor, he continued his support for this legislative device, even though it covers only a small portion of legislation.

References

Abramowitz, A. I. 1994. "Issue Evolution Reconsidered: Racial Attitudes and Partisanship in the U.S. Electorate." *American Journal of Political Science* 38: 1–24.

Achen, C. H. 1986. *The Statistical Analysis of Quasi-Experiments.* Berkeley and Los Angeles: University of California Press.

Aldrich, J. H. 1993. "Presidential Selection." In *Researching the Presidency: Vital Questions, New Approaches,* ed. G. C. Edwards III, J. H. Kessel, and B. A. Rockman. Pittsburgh: University of Pittsburgh Press.

Allison, G. 1971. *Essence of Decision.* Boston: Little, Brown.

Anderson, F. L., et al. 1966. *Legislative Roll-Call Analysis.* Evanston, IL: Northwestern University Press.

Anderson, J. 1975. *Public Policy-Making.* New York: Praeger.

Barber, J. D., ed. 1974. *Choosing the President.* Englewood Cliffs, NJ: Prentice-Hall.

Barber, J. D. 1980. *Pursuit of the Presidency.* Englewood Cliffs, NJ: Prentice-Hall.

Barber, J. D. 1992. *Presidential Character.* 4th ed. Englewood Cliffs, NJ: Prentice-Hall.

Baumgartner, F., and B. D. Jones. 1993. *Agendas and Instability in American Politics.* Chicago: University of Chicago Press.

Beck, N. 1982. "Parties, Administrations, and American Macroeconomic Outcomes." *American Political Science Review* 76: 83–93.

Bond, J., and R. Fleisher. 1980. "Limits of Presidential Popularity as a Source of Influence in the House." *Legislative Studies Quarterly* 5: 69–78.

Bond, J., and R. Fleisher. 1984. "Presidential Popularity and Congressional Voting." *Western Political Quarterly* 37: 291–306.

Bond, J., and R. Fleisher. 1990. *The President in the Legislative Arena.* Chicago: University of Chicago Press.

Bond, J., et al. 1991. "Implications for Research in Studying Presidential-Congressional Relations." In *The Two Presidencies: A Quarter Century Assessment,* ed. S. A. Shull. Chicago: Nelson-Hall.

Bond, J., R. Fleisher, and G. S. Krutz. 1996. "Empirical Findings on Presidential-Congressional Relations." In *Rivals for Power: Presidential-Congressional Relations,* ed. J. A. Thurber. Washington, DC: CQ Press.

Borrelli, S. A., and G. L. Simmons. 1992. "Congressional Responsiveness to Presidential Popularity: The Electoral Context." *Political Behavior* 15: 93–112.

Campbell, A. 1960. *The American Voter.* New York: John Wiley and Sons.

Campbell, C., and B. Rockman, eds. 1991. *The Bush Presidency: First Appraisals.* Chatham, NJ: Chatham House.

Chamberlain, L. H. 1946. "President, Congress, and Legislation." *Political Science Quarterly* 61: 42–60.

Chandler, M. A., W. M. Chandler, and D. Vogler. 1974. "Policy Analysis and the Search for Theory." *American Politics Quarterly* 2: 107–18.

Clausen, A. R. 1973. *How Congressmen Decide: A Policy Focus.* New York: St. Martin's Press.

Clausen, A. R., and C. E. Van Horn. 1977. "Congressional Response to a Decade of Change: 1963–1972." *Journal of Politics* 39: 624–66.

Codification of Presidential Proclamations and Executive Orders. Irregular. Washington, DC: United States Government Printing Office.

Cohen, J. E. 1980. "Presidential Personality and Political Behavior." *Presidential Studies Quarterly* 10: 588–99.

Cohen, J. E. [1982] 1991. "Historical Reassessment of Wildavsky's 'Two Presidencies' Thesis." In *The Two Presidencies: A Quarter Century Assessment,* ed. S. A. Shull. Chicago: Nelson-Hall.

Congress and the Nation. 1981. Vol. 5. Washington, DC: Congressional Quarterly.

Congressional Roll Call (annual). Washington, DC: Congressional Quarterly.

Congressional Quarterly Almanac (annual). Washington, DC: Congressional Quarterly.

Congressional Quarterly Weekly Reports. Washington, DC: Congressional Quarterly.

Cooper, P. 1986. "By Order of the President: Administration by Executive Order and Proclamation." *Administration and Society* 18: 233–62.

Covington, C. R. 1987. "Staying Private: Gaining Congressional Support for Unpublicized Presidential Preferences on Roll Call Votes." *Journal of Politics* 49: 737–55.

Covington, C. R., et al. 1995. "A Presidency-Augmented Model of Presidential Success on House Roll Call Votes." *American Journal of Political Science* 39: 1001–24.

Cox, G. W., and S. Kernell, eds. 1991. *Politics of Divided Government.* Boulder, CO: Westview Press.

Cox, G. W., and M. D. McCubbins. 1991. "Divided Control of Fiscal Policy." In *Politics of Divided Government,* ed. G. W. Cox and S. Kernell. Boulder, CO: Westview Press.

Cronin, T. 1980. *State of the Presidency.* 2d ed. Boston: Little, Brown.

Cronin, T., and R. Tugwell, eds. 1977. *The Presidency Reappraised.* 2d ed. New York: Praeger.

Cutler, L. 1988. "Some Reflections on Divided Government." *Presidential Studies Quarterly* 18: 485–92.

Dahl, R. A. 1950. *Congress and Foreign Policy.* New York: Harcourt Brace.

Dahl, R. A. 1963. *Modern Political Analysis.* Englewood Cliffs, NJ: Prentice-Hall.

Destler, I. M. 1974. *Presidents, Bureaucrats, and Foreign Policy.* Princeton, NJ: Princeton University Press.

Dodd, L., and B. Oppenheimer, eds. 1981. *Congress Reconsidered,* 2d ed. Washington, DC: Congressional Quarterly Press.

Donovan, J. C. 1970. *The Policy Makers.* New York: Pegasus.

Donovan, J. C. 1974. *The Cold Warriors.* Lexington, MA: D. C. Heath.

Durant, R. F. 1992. *Administrative Presidency Revisited.* Albany: State University of New York Press.

Edelman, M. J. 1974. "The Politics of Persuasion." In *Choosing the President,* ed. J. D. Barber. Englewood Cliffs, NJ: Prentice-Hall.

Edwards, G. C., III. 1980. *Presidential Influence in Congress.* San Francisco: W. H. Freeman.

Edwards, G. C., III. 1985. "Measuring Presidential Success in Congress: Alternative Approaches." *Journal of Politics* 47: 667–85.

Edwards, G. C., III. [1986] 1991. "Two Presidencies: A Re-evaluation." In *The Two Presidencies: A Quarter Century Assessment,* ed. S. A. Shull. Chicago: Nelson-Hall.

Edwards, G. C., III. 1989. *At the Margins: Presidential Leadership of Congress.* New Haven, CT: Yale University Press.

Edwards, G. C., III. 1991. "Response to Sullivan's 'The Bank Account Presidency.'" *American Journal of Political Science* 34: 724–29.

Edwards, G. C., III, A. Barrett, and J. Peake. 1997. "The Legislative Impact of Divided Government." *American Journal of Political Science* 41: 545–63.

Edwards, G. C., III, J. H. Kessel, and B. A. Rockman, eds. 1993. *Researching the Presidency: Vital Questions, New Approaches.* Pittsburgh: University of Pittsburgh Press.

Edwards, G. C., III, and S. J. Wayne, eds. 1983. *Studying the Presidency.* Knoxville: University of Tennessee Press.

Eisner, M. A., and K. J. Meier. 1990. "Presidential Control versus Bureaucratic Power." *American Journal of Political Science* 34: 269–87.

Federalist Papers. 1956. New York: New American Library.

Federal Register (daily). Washington, DC: United States Government Printing Office.

Fenno, R. F. 1973. *Congressmen in Committees.* Boston: Little, Brown.

Fett, P. J. 1994. "Presidential Legislative Priorities and Legislators' Voting Decisions." *Journal of Politics* 56: 502–12.

Fiorina, M. P. 1996. *Divided Government.* 2d ed. Needham Heights, MA: Allyn and Bacon.

Fiorina, M. P., and R. G. Noll. 1979. "Majority Rule Models and Legislative Elections." *Journal of Politics* 41: 1081–104.

Fisher, L. 1972. *The President and Congress.* New York: Free Press.

Flaxbeard, J. M. 1983. "Presidential Policy Making: The Use of Executive Orders and Presidential Support on Civil Rights Issues." Presented at the annual meeting of the Southern Political Science Association, Birmingham, Alabama.

Fleisher, R., and J. Bond. 1983. "Assessing Presidential Support in the House." *Journal of Politics* 49: 745–58.

Fleisher, R., and J. Bond. [1988] 1991. "Are There Two Presidencies?" In *The Two Presidencies: A Quarter Century Assessment,* ed. S. A. Shull. Chicago: Nelson-Hall.

Froman, L. E. 1968. "The Categorization of Policy Contents." In *Political Science and Public Policy,* ed. A. Ranney. Chicago: Markham Publishing.

Fry, B. R., and R. F. Winters. 1970. "Politics of Redistribution." *American Political Science Review* 64: 508–22.

Gallagher, H. G. 1977. "The President, Congress, and Legislation." In *The Presidency Reappraised,* 2d ed., ed. T. Cronin and R. Tugwell. New York: Praeger.

Garand, J. C., and D. A. Gross. 1982. "Toward a Theory of Bureaucratic Compliance with Presidential Directions." *Presidential Studies Quarterly* 12: 195–207.

Gibson, M. 1995. "Issues, Coalitions, and Divided Government." *Congress and the President* 22: 155–66.

Gleiber, D. W., and S. A. Shull. 1992. "Presidential Influence in the Policymaking Process." *Western Political Quarterly* 41: 441–67.

Goldfinger, J., and S. A. Shull. 1995. "Presidential Influence on Major Legislation." Presented at the annual meeting of the American Political Science Association, Chicago.

Gomez, B. T., and S. A. Shull. 1995. "Presidential Decision Making: Explaining the Use of Executive Orders." Presented at the annual meeting of the Southern Political Science Association, Tampa, Florida.

Greenberg, G. D., et al. 1977. "Developing Public Policy Theory: Perspectives from Empirical Research." *American Political Science Review* 71: 1532–43.

Gurr, T. R. 1972. *Polimetrics: An Introduction to Quantitative Macropolitics.* Englewood Cliffs, NJ: Prentice-Hall.

Hager, G. L., and T. Sullivan. 1994. "President-Centered and Presidency-Centered Explanations of Presidential Public Activity." *American Journal of Political Science* 38: 1079–103.

Hall, R. L. 1987. "Participation and Purpose in Committee Decision Making." *American Political Science Review* 81: 105–128.

Hammond, T. H., and J. M. Fraser. 1980. "Faction Size, the Conservative Coalition, and the Determinants of Presidential Success in Congress." Presented at the annual meeting of the American Political Science Association, Washington, DC.

Hammond, T. H., and J. M. Fraser. 1984a. "Judging Presidential Performance on House and Senate Roll Calls." *Polity* 16: 624–46.

Hammond, T. H., and J. M. Fraser. 1984b. "Studying Presidential Performance in Congress." *Political Methodology* 10: 211–44.

Hargrove, E. C. 1974. *The Power of the Modern Presidency.* Philadelphia: Temple University Press.

Hayes, M. T. 1978. "Semi-Sovereign Pressure Groups: A Critique of Current Theory and an Alternative Typology." *Journal of Politics* 40: 134–61.

Hayes, S., et al. 1984. "Presidential Support among Senatorial Leaders and Followers." *American Politics Quarterly* 12: 195–209.

Heckathorn, D. D., and S. M. Maser. 1990. "The Contractual Architecture of Public Policy: A Critical Reconstruction of Lowi's Typology." *Journal of Politics* 52: 1101–23.

Hilsman, R. 1968. *To Move a Nation: The Politics of Foreign Policy in the Administration of John F. Kennedy.* New York: Dell.

Hinckley, B. 1994. *Less than Meets the Eye.* Chicago: University of Chicago Press.

Holsti, O. R., and J. N. Rosenau. 1984. *American Leadership in World Affairs: Vietnam and the Breakdown of Consensus.* Boston: G. Allen and Unwin.

Huntington, S. P. 1961. *The Common Defense: Strategic Programs in National Politics.* New York: Columbia University Press.

Johannes, J. R. 1972a. *Policy Innovation in Congress.* Morristown, NJ: General Learning Press.

Johannes, J. R. 1972b. "Where Does the Buck Stop? Congress, President, and the Responsibility for Legislative Initiation." *Western Political Quarterly* 25: 396–415.

Jones, C. O. 1984. *An Introduction to the Study of Public Policy.* 3d ed. Monterey, CA: Brooks/Cole.

Jones, C. O. 1994. *Presidency in a Separated System.* Washington, DC: Brookings Institution.

Jones, C. O. 1995. *Separate but Equal Branches.* Chatham, NJ: Chatham House.

Kelly, S. Q. 1993. "Divided We Govern?: A Reassessment." *Polity* 35: 475–90.

Kerbel, M. R. 1991. *Beyond Persuasion: Organizational Efficiency and Presidential Power.* Albany: State University of New York Press.

Kernell, S. 1986. *Going Public: New Strategies of Presidential Leadership.* Washington, DC: CQ Press.

Kerwin, C. M. 1994. *Rulemaking: How Government Agencies Write Law and Make Policy.* Washington, DC: CQ Press.

Kessel, J. H. 1974. "Parameters of Presidential Politics." *Social Science Quarterly* 55: 8–24.

Kessel, J. H. 1975. *The Domestic Presidency: Decision-Making in the White House.* North Scituate, MA: Duxbury Press.

Kessel, J. H. 1977. "Seasons of Presidential Politics." *Social Science Quarterly* 58: 418–35.

Kessel, J. H. 1984. *Presidential Parties.* Homewood, IL: Dorsey Press.

Kettl, D. F. 1992. *Deficit Politics.* New York: Macmillan.

Key, V. O. 1964. *Politics, Parties, and Pressure Groups.* New York: Crowell.

King, G. 1986. "The Significance of Roll Calls in Voting Bodies: A Model and Statistical Estimation." *Social Science Research* 15: 135–52.

King, G., and L. Ragsdale. 1988. *The Elusive Executive: Discovering Statistical Patterns in the Presidency.* Washington, DC: CQ Press.

Kingdon, J. W. 1984. *Agendas, Alternatives, and Public Policies.* Boston: Little, Brown.

Koenig, L. W. 1975. *The Chief Executive.* New York: Harcourt Brace Jovanovich.

Laurance, E. J. 1976. "Changing Role of Congress in Defense Policy Making." *Journal of Conflict Resolution* 20: 213–53.

LeLoup, L. T., and S. A. Shull. [1979a] 1991. "Congress versus the President, 'The Two Presidencies Reconsidered.'" In *The Two Presidencies: A Quarter Century Assessment,* ed. S. A. Shull. Chicago: Nelson-Hall.

LeLoup, L. T., and S. A. Shull. 1979b. "Dimensions of Presidential Policy Making." In *The Presidency: Studies in Public Policy,* ed. S. A. Shull and L. T. LeLoup. Brunswick, OH: King's Court Communications.

LeLoup, L. T., and S. A. Shull. 1993. *Congress and the President: The Policy Connection.* Belmont, CA: Wadsworth.

Light, P. 1982. *President's Agenda: Domestic Policy Choice from Kennedy to Carter.* Baltimore: Johns Hopkins University Press.

Light, P. 1992. *Forging Legislation.* New York: W. W. Norton.

Lindblom, C. E. 1959. "The 'Science' of Muddling Through." *Public Administration Review* 19: 79–88.

Lindsay, J. M., and R. B. Ripley. 1993. "How Congress Influences Foreign and Defense." In *Congressional Resurgence in Foreign Policy,* ed. R. B. Ripley and J. M. Lindsay. Ann Arbor: University of Michigan Press.

Lindsay, J. M., and W. P. Steger. 1993. "Two Presidencies in Future Research." *Congress and the Presidency* 20: 103–17.

Lockerbie, B., and S. A. Borrelli. 1989. "Getting Inside the Beltway: Perceptions of Presidential Skill and Success in Congress." *British Journal of Political Science* 19: 97–106.

Lowi, T. J. 1964. "American Business, Public Policy, Case Studies, and Political Theory." *World Politics* 16: 677–715.

Lowi, T. J. 1970. "Decision-Making vs. Policy Making: Toward an Antidote for Technocracy." *Public Administration Review* 30: 314–25.

Lowi, T. J. 1972. "Four Systems of Policy, Politics, and Choice." *Public Administration Review* 32: 298–310.

Lowi, T. J. 1985. *The Personal President: Power Invested, Promise Unfulfilled.* Ithaca, NY: Cornell University Press.

MacRae, D. 1970. *Issues and Parties in Legislative Voting: Methods of Statistical Analysis.* New York: Harper and Row.

Manley, J. F. 1971. "Rise of Congress in Foreign Policy Making." *Annals* 397: 60–70.

Manning, B. 1977. "Congress, the Executive, and Intermestic Affairs: Three Proposals." *Foreign Affairs* 55: 306–24.

Mayhew, D. R. 1966. *Party Loyalty among Congressmen: The Difference between Democrats and Republicans, 1947–1962.* Cambridge: Harvard University Press.

Mayhew, D. R. 1992. *Divided We Govern.* New Haven, CT: Yale University Press.

Mayhew, D. R. 1995. "Clinton, the 103rd Congress, and Unified Party Control." Yale University. Mimeograph.

McConnell, G. 1976. *The Modern Presidency.* New York: St. Martin's Press.

McCubbins, M. D. 1991. "Government on Lay-Away: Federal Spending and Deficits under Divided Party Control." In *The Politics of Divided Government,* ed. G. W. Cox and S. Kernell. Boulder, CO: Westview Press.

Mezey, M. 1989. *Congress, the President, and Public Policy.* Boulder, CO: Westview.

Miroff, B. 1976. *Pragmatic Illusions: The Presidential Politics of John F. Kennedy.* New York: McKay.

Moe, R. C., and S. Teel. 1970. "Congress as Policy Maker: A Necessary Reappraisal." *Political Science Quarterly* 85: 443–70.

Moe, T. M. 1982. "Regulatory Performance and Presidential Administration." *American Journal of Political Science* 26: 197–224.

Morgan, R. P. 1970. *The President and Civil Rights: Policy Making by Executive Order.* New York: St. Martin's Press.

Mouw, C., and M. MacKuen. 1992. "The Strategic Configuration, Personal Influence, and Presidential Power in Congress." *Western Political Quarterly* 41: 579–608.

Nathan, R. P. 1983. *The Administrative Presidency.* 2d ed. New York: John Wiley and Sons.

National Journal (selected issues). Washington, DC: Government Research Corporation.

Neustadt, R. E. 1955. "Presidency and Legislation: Planning the President's Program." *American Political Science Review* 49: 980–1021.

Neustadt, R. E. 1960. *Presidential Power: The Politics of Leadership.* New York: John Wiley and Sons.

Neustadt, R. E. 1973. "Politicians and Bureaucrats." In *The Congress and America's Future,* 2d ed., ed. D. Truman. Englewood Cliffs, NJ: Prentice-Hall.

Oldfield, D., and A. Wildavsky. [1989] 1991. "Reconsidering the Two Presidencies." In *The Two Presidencies: A Quarter Century Assessment,* ed. S. A. Shull. Chicago: Nelson-Hall.

Orfield, G. 1975. *Congressional Power: Congress and Social Change.* New York: Harcourt Brace Jovanovich.

Ornstein, N. J., et al. 1996. *Vital Statistics on Congress 1995–1996.* Washington, DC: Congressional Quarterly.

Ostrom, E. 1980. "Is It B or Not-B? That Is the Question." *Social Science Quarterly* 61: 198–202.

Parker, G. L., and S. L. Parker. 1985. *Functions in House Committees.* Knoxville: University of Tennessee Press.

Patterson, S. C., and G. A. Caldeira. 1988. "Party Voting in the U.S. Congress." *British Journal of Political Science* 18: 111–31.

Peppers, D. A. [1975] 1991. "Two Presidencies: Eight Years Later." In *The Two Presidencies: A Quarter Century Assessment,* ed. S. A. Shull. Chicago: Nelson-Hall.

Peterson, M. A. 1990. *Legislating Together.* Cambridge: Harvard University Press.

Peterson, P. E., ed. 1994. *The President, the Congress, and the Making of Foreign Policy.* Norman: University of Oklahoma Press.

Petrocik, J. R. 1991. "Divided Government: Is It All in the Campaigns?" In *The Politics of Divided Government,* ed. G. W. Cox and S. Kernell. Boulder, CO: Westview Press.

Polsby, N. W. 1969. "Policy Analysis and Congress." *Public Policy* 18: 61–74.

Pomper, G. M. 1980. *Elections in America.* 2d ed. New York: Longman.

Price, D. E. 1972. *Who Makes the Laws? Creativity and Power in Senate Committees.* Cambridge, MA: Schenkman Publishing.

Pritchard, A. 1983. "Presidents Do Influence Voting in the U. S. Congress." *Legislative Studies Quarterly* 8: 691–711.

Pritchard, A. 1986. "An Evaluation of C.Q.'s Presidential Support Scores." *American Journal of Political Science* 30: 480–95.

Public Papers of the Presidents of the United States (annual). Washington, DC: United States Government Printing Office.

Ragsdale, L. 1993. *Presidential Politics.* Boston: Houghton-Mifflin.

Ragsdale, L. 1996. *Vital Statistics on the Presidency.* Washington, DC: CQ Press.

Ranney, A., ed. 1968. *Political Science and Public Policy.* Chicago: Markham Publishing.

Redford, E. S. 1969. *Democracy in the Administrative State.* New York: Oxford University Press.

Renka, R. D., and B. J. Jones. 1991. "The 'Two Presidencies' during the Reagan and Bush Administrations." In *The Two Presidencies: A Quarter Century Assessment,* ed. S. A. Shull. Chicago: Nelson-Hall.

Ripley, R. B. 1969. "Power in the Post-World War II Senate." *Journal of Politics* 31: 465–92.

Ripley, R. B. 1972. *The Politics of Economic and Human Resource Development.* Indianapolis: Bobbs-Merrill.

Ripley, R. B. 1979. "Carter and Congress." In *The Presidency: Studies in Public Policy,* ed. S. A. Shull and L. T. LeLoup. Brunswick, OH: King's Court Communications.

Ripley, R. B., and G. A. Franklin. 1986. *Bureaucracy and Policy Implementation.* 2d ed. Homewood, IL: Dorsey Press.

Ripley, R. B., and G. A. Franklin. 1991. *Congress, the Bureaucracy, and Public Policy.* 5th ed. Belmont, CA: Wadsworth Publishing.

Ripley, R. B., and J. M. Lindsay, eds. 1993. *Congressional Resurgence in Foreign Policy.* Ann Arbor: University of Michigan Press.

Rivers, D., and N. L. Rose. 1985. "Passing the President's Program." *American Journal of Political Science* 29: 183–96.

Robinson, J. A. 1967. *Congress and Foreign Policy-Making: A Study in Legislative Influence and Initiative.* Rev. ed. Homewood, IL: Dorsey Press.

Rockman, B. A. 1991. "The Leadership Style of George Bush." In *The Bush Presidency: First Appraisals,* ed. C. Campbell and B. A. Rockman. Chatham, NJ: Chatham House.

Rohde, D. W. 1994. "Presidential Support in the House of Representatives." In *The President, the Congress, and the Making of Foreign Policy,* ed. P. E. Peterson. Norman: University of Oklahoma Press.

Rossiter, C. 1956. *The American Presidency.* New York: Harcourt, Brace.

Salisbury, R. 1968. "The Analysis of Public Policy: A Search for Theories and Roles." In *Political Science and Public Policy,* ed. A. Ranney. Chicago: Markham Publishing.

Salisbury, R., and J. Heinz. 1970. "A Theory of Policy Analysis and Some Preliminary Applications." In *Policy Analysis in Political Science,* ed. I. Sharkansky. Chicago: Markham Publishing.

Schlesinger, A. Jr. 1986. *The Cycles of American History.* Boston: Houghton-Mifflin.

Schwarz, J. E., and L. E. Shaw. 1976. *The United States Congress in Comparative Perspective.* Hinsdale, IL: Dryden Press.

Sharkansky, I., ed. 1970. *Policy Analysis in Political Science.* Chicago: Markham Publishing.

Shaw, T. C., and S. A. Shull. 1996. "Beyond Divided Government: Explaining Vote Controversy on Important Legislation." Presented at the annual meeting of the American Political Science Association, San Francisco.

Shull, S. A. 1979. *Presidential Policy Making: An Analysis.* Brunswick, OH: King's Court Communications.

Shull, S. A. 1981. "Assessing Measures of Presidential-Congressional Interaction." *Presidential Studies Quarterly* 11: 151–57.

Shull, S. A. 1983. *Domestic Policy Formation.* Westport, CT: Greenwood Press.

Shull, S. A. 1989. *The President and Civil Rights Policy.* Westport, CT: Greenwood Press.

Shull, S. A., ed. 1991. *The Two Presidencies: A Quarter Century Assessment.* Chicago: Nelson-Hall.

Shull, S. A. 1993. *A Kinder, Gentler Racism? The Reagan-Bush Civil Rights Legacy.* Armonk, NY: M. E. Sharp.

Shull, S. A. 1994. "Conceptual and Measurement Concerns about Lindsay's and Steger's 'The Two Presidencies in Future Research.'" *Congress and the Presidency* 21: 159–62.

Shull, S. A., and D. Garland. 1996. "Presidential Influence versus Agency Discretion: A Test of Three Models." *Policy Studies Review* 14: 49–70.

Shull, S. A., and D. W. Gleiber. 1994. "Testing a Dynamic Process of Policy Making in Civil Rights." *Social Science Journal* 31: 53–67.

Shull, S. A., and D. W. Gleiber. 1995. "Presidential Cycles in Civil Rights Policy Making." *Presidential Studies Quarterly* 25: 429–46.

Shull, S. A., and M. F. Klemm. 1987. "Amendments versus All Votes: A Comparison of Assertiveness and Controversy in Congress." *Southeastern Political Review* 15: 139–58.

Shull, S. A., and L. T. LeLoup, eds. 1979. *The Presidency: Studies in Public Policy.* Brunswick, OH: King's Court Communications.

Shull, S. A., and L. T. LeLoup. [1981] 1991. "Comment on Lee Sigelman's 'Reassessing the 'Two Presidencies' Thesis.'" In *The Two Presidencies: A Quarter Century Assessment,* ed. S. A. Shull. Chicago: Nelson-Hall.

Shull, S. A., and J. Vanderleeuw. 1987. "What Do Key Votes Measure?" *Legislative Studies Quarterly* 12: 573–82.

Shull, S. A., et al. 1985. "Establishing Dimensionality in U. S. Foreign Policy." *Southeastern Political Review* 13: 153–68.

Sigelman, L. [1979] 1991. "Reassessing the 'Two Presidencies' Thesis." In *The Two Presidencies: A Quarter Century Assessment,* ed. S. A. Shull. Chicago: Nelson-Hall.

Sinclair, B. 1981. "Agenda and Alignment Change: The House of Representatives, 1925–1978." In *Congress Reconsidered,* 2d ed., ed. L. Dodd and B. Oppenheimer. Washington, DC: Congressional Quarterly Press.

Sperlich, P. W. 1975. "Bargaining and Overload: An Essay on Power." In *Perspectives on the Presidency,* ed. A. Wildavsky. Boston: Little, Brown.

Spitzer, R. 1983. *Presidency and Public Policy.* Tuscaloosa: University of Alabama Press.

Spitzer, R. 1988. *The President's Veto.* Albany: State University of New York Press.

Spitzer, R. 1993. *The President and Congress.* New York: McGraw-Hill.

Steinberger, P. J. 1980. "Typologies of Public Policy: Meaning Construction and the Policy Process." *Social Science Quarterly* 61: 185–97.

Sullivan, T. 1991a. "A Matter of Fact: The Two Presidencies Thesis Revisited." In *The Two Presidencies: A Quarter Century Assessment,* ed. S. A. Shull. Chicago: Nelson-Hall.

Sullivan, T. 1991b. "The Bank Account Presidency." *American Journal of Political Science* 35: 686–723.

Sullivan, T. 1991c. "Rejoinder to Edward's *Presidential Influence in Congress.*" *American Journal of Political Science* 35: 730–37.

Sundquist, J. L. 1968. *Politics and Policy: The Eisenhower, Kennedy, and Johnson Years.* Washington, DC: Brookings Institution.

Sundquist, J. L. 1981. *Decline and Resurgence in Congress.* Washington, DC: Brookings Institution.

Sundquist, J. L. 1992. *Constitutional Reform and Effective Government. Rev. ed.* Washington, DC: Brookings Institution.

Tatalovich, R., and B. Daynes. 1979. "Towards a Paradigm to Explain Presidential Power." *Presidential Studies Quarterly* 9: 428–40.

Thomas, N. C. 1977. "Studying the Presidency: Where Do We Go from Here?" *Presidential Studies Quarterly* 7: 169–74.

Thurber, J. A., ed. 1991. *Divided Democracy.* Washington, DC: Congressional Quarterly.

Thurber, J. A., ed. 1996. *Rivals for Power: Presidential-Congressional Relations.* Washington, DC: CQ Press.

Tocqueville, A. [1835] 1990. *Democracy in America.* Trans. Henry Reeve, ed. Phillips Bradley. New York: Vintage Books.

Truman, D. 1981. *The Congress and America's Future.* 2d ed. Englewood Cliffs, NJ: Prentice-Hall.

Tufte, E. R. 1978. *Political Control of the Economy.* Princeton, NJ: Princeton University Press.

Uslaner, E. M. 1993. *Decline of Comity in Congress.* Ann Arbor: University of Michigan Press.

Uslaner, E. M., and R. E. Weber. 1975. "The 'Politics' of Redistribution: Toward a Model of the Policy-Making Process in the American States." *American Politics Quarterly* 3: 131–69.

Utter, G. H., and P. J. Cooper. 1995. "The Clinton Administration and Presidential Power Tools: Political Tactics and Administrative Realities." Presented at the annual meeting of the Southern Political Science Association, Tampa, Florida.

Vogler, D. J. 1977. *The Politics of Congress.* 2d ed. Boston: Allyn and Bacon.

Waterman, R. 1989. *Presidential Influence and the Administrative State.* Knoxville: University of Tennessee Press.

Watson, R. A. 1993. *Presidential Vetoes and Public Policy.* Lawrence: University Press of Kansas.

Wayne, S. J. 1978. *Legislative Presidency.* New York: Harper and Row.

Weekly Compilation of Presidential Documents. Washington, DC: United States Government Printing Office.

Who's Who in Congress (annual). Washington, DC: Congressional Quarterly.

Wildavsky, A. [1966] 1991. "Two Presidencies." In *The Two Presidencies: A Quarter Century Assessment,* ed. S. A. Shull. Chicago: Nelson-Hall.

Wildavsky, A. 1975. *Perspectives on the Presidency.* Boston: Little, Brown.

Wildavsky, A. 1979. *Speaking Truth to Power: The Art and Craft of Policy Analysis.* Boston: Little, Brown.

Wildavsky, A. 1991. Foreword to *The Two Presidencies: A Quarter Century Assessment,* ed. S. A. Shull. Chicago: Nelson-Hall.

Wilson, J. Q. 1973. *Political Organizations.* New York: Basic Books.

Wilson, W. 1885. *Congressional Government: A Study in American Politics.* Boston: Houghton-Mifflin.

Wilson, W. 1908. *Constitutional Government in the United States.* New York: Columbia University Press.

Wood, B. D. 1988. "Principals, Bureaucrats, and Responsiveness in Clean Air Enforcements." *American Political Science Review* 12: 213–34.

Wood, B. D., and J. E. Anderson. 1993. "Politics of U. S. Anti-Trust Regulation." *American Journal of Political Science* 37: 1–39.

Wood, B. D., and R. W. Waterman. 1991. "Dynamics of Political Control of the Bureaucracy." *American Political Science Review* 85: 801–28.

Zeidenstein, H. [1981] 1991. "The Two Presidencies Thesis Is Alive and Well . . . " In *The Two Presidencies: A Quarter Century Assessment,* ed. S. A. Shull. Chicago: Nelson-Hall.

Index

activities. *See* executive order issuance; political time; presidential position taking; support; vote controversy

agenda setting, 1, 6, 124; 1994–95 shift in, 10; increased role of Congress in, 7, 14–15; presidential influence on, 8

aggregation, 11–12

agriculture: and congressional support, 94; as distributive policy, 5; under divided government, 10; executive orders on, 107, 108; lack of agreement on, 134; and policy area typology, 35; position taking on, 49, 54, 55, 62–63

amendments: characteristics of votes on, 122; frequency, 48; frequency by chamber, 70, 72; increase in numbers of, 32; as measure of controversy, 41; numbers of under individual presidents, 74, 79

Americans for Democratic Action (ADA) index, 67, 150

Barber, James David, on cycles in American history, 12

Barrett, Andrew: on effect of divided government, 66; on failed legislation, 41

baseline models of congressional voting behavior, 87

Beck, Nathaniel, on presidential policy agendas, 39

Bond, Jon: on committee behavior, 7; on multivariate analysis of presidential-congressional relations, 9; on partisan voting, 66; on two presidencies thesis, 18–19

Bosnia intervention, 148

boxscore (CQ), 31, 132; as database, 26; definition of, 33; as measure of legislative success, 70, 81–82; research project on, 151; and two presidencies thesis, 18

budgeting, 8, 132; and congressional participation, 126

bureaucrats, role in policy, 3

Bush, George: congressional support for, 91, 95; executive order issuance, 102, 104, 105; votes on important legislation under, 42–43

Carter, Jimmy: and civil rights policies, 100; congressional support for, 90, 93; and executive order issuance, 102, 107, 109; high assertiveness rating of, 120; votes on important legislation under, 42–43

chamber. *See* House of Representatives; Senate

chamber differences: and roll call votes, 67–68; in vote controversy, 78

Chamberlain, L. H., on congressional role, 2

Chandler, Marsha, critique of Lowi typology, 27

Chandler, William, critique of Lowi typology, 27

checks and balances. *See* separation of powers

child care, congressional leadership in, 3

civil rights: and executive orders, 100, 101–2, 149; individual presidencies and, 38; policy-making cycles on, 37